D1499637

MEDITATION

DEDICATION

MEDITATION

A Step Beyond with Edgar Cayce

BY M. E. PENNY BAKER

Foreword by Hugh Lynn Cayce

1973

Doubleday & Company, Inc., Garden City, New York

ISBN: 0-385-00984-4
Library of Congress Catalog Card Number 72–96227
Copyright © 1973 by M. E. Penny Baker
All Rights Reserved
Printed in the United States of America
First Edition

This book is dedicated with
love to three of the most
important people in my life:
my mother; my son, Jamie;
and Elton.

"Read a portion, think on
same; that these words are
not mere combinations of
ideas expressed by a writer
from those activities
of an idealist, but that
they are as living water,
as the bread of life
to the body-mind itself;
as those things, expressions
and experiences that may
be a part and parcel of
the entity itself."

1053-1

Foreword

Of all the data in the Edgar Cayce readings, the material on meditation is for many seekers the most exciting, the most helpful and the most difficult. It is the simplicity of the Edgar Cayce suggestions which may lead one to say too early, "There can't be much to this, it is too easy."

Perhaps it is at this point that Penny Baker makes a real contribution to the growing number of books on various subjects dealt with in the Edgar Cayce data. In this book on meditation she brings clarity and succinctness to the suggestions for this daily discipline of the mind and body. The beginner can follow her directions easily. However, beyond the straightforward practicality of the procedure which is outlined, she goes on to open the door to deeper understanding of such subjects as: the importance of the seven endocrine centers identified with the Eastern concept of the chakra; the value of group meditations both in focusing and magnifying spiritual energy and the protective power of the group energy; interesting warnings regarding the wrong use of the energies released through meditation by building negative thought patterns; and the opportunities which are aroused through the dicipline of meditation.

In my opinion, the practice of meditation is especially valuable for people in our present-day society. Our lives are filled with pressures of a thousand different kinds; noise, speed, food of questionable value, pollution, conflicts arising out of our differences with social structures, a hundred different faces of fear, frustrations with our vocational patterns, and on and on. Meditation is a way to inner peace, a road to a new plateau of consciousness, a way to the discovery of "the kingdom within." Penny Baker has caught the urgency and the excitement of Edgar Cayce's admonition to find "this secret place of the most high." Try walking this path and you may never be the same again.

Hugh Lynn Cayce

Acknowledgments

My deepest thanks to Rose De Vito, Tony's wife, for the gift of Thomas Sugrue's book of *There Is a River*. Without Mrs. De Vito's gift, many things would not have been possible for me. A debt of gratitude is owed to Lucille Kahn and Ruth Hagy Brod for being the channels when needed. Thank you, Margo Canton, for listening to all of my theories when no one else would. Thanks to Hugh Lynn Cayce and others at A. R. E. for their patience and understanding. Thanks to William Peter Langhurst for his helpful suggestions. And to the members of that first study group in New York—Neal Edwards; Eleanor Harrington; Ed Rundquist; Jim Wimer; Betty Rubenstein; Terance Benson, and Alice Essessian, my gratitude for the growth and knowledge which came to all of us.

Introduction

From 1901 to 1945, Edgar Cayce, America's foremost clairvoyant, assumed a self-induced trancelike state approximately 16,000 times. The result was nearly 15,000 recorded psychic readings. The readings were in response to questions asked by the many individuals who sought the aid of Cayce on problems ranging from vocation, health, marital difficulties, birth, death, on through to the spiritual side of life.

Edgar Cayce was born in Hopkinsville, Kentucky, in 1877 and died at Virginia Beach, Virginia, in 1945. Always a deeply religious man, Cayce had difficulty at first in accepting the philosophy pertaining to reincarnation and some of the other spiritual aspects which came through the readings. However, once he had decided it all fit a pattern and made sense, he gave his life to the work.

The Association for Research and Enlightenment at

Virginia Beach, Virginia, was founded to preserve and further the Cayce work. At the A. R. E. library, the many readings are indexed and catalogued, and are available for study to anyone seeking. Hundreds of thousands of people come from all over the world each year to research and study the Cayce readings for a meaning to life and its many complexities.

A number of those who come to A. R. E. do so because of their interest in the health readings; however, they find they are increasingly drawn to the spiritual readings. Frequently, as a result of the newly aroused interest, they become curious about meditation. It is sincerely hoped by this writer that these people, and others searching for Truth, will find some of their questions answered in this book, which is based upon the Cayce philosophy of "meditation" and "look within."

The excerpts from the Cayce readings are designated by the number of the reading set in parenthesis. The readings cannot be scanned but must be studied if one is to fully understand the meaning of them. At times, they may seem complex, even contradictory, but for those who will take the time to study the readings, there is a wealth of knowledge buried in the archaic language.

Contents

MEDITATION

Chapter I

WHAT IS MEDITATION?

For many the time has come when they must face themselves and make peace with the inner self. Society has become a very complex, often terrifying experience for many individuals. What we see, hear, and find, frequently leads to personal confusion for some people. Seemingly, there is no place to turn for help.

In this era of lightning-like communication, turning in to oneself has become alien; many have forgotten how. Yet from *within* comes the true answer for life and its many problems. It is within oneself that each individual can meet and know God. And who is better qualified than God to know what is best for each of us? In creating man, God bestowed upon him the gift of free will. But even with this divine gift each of us has a constant need for help and guidance.

The path to divine guidance can be found in meditation. To be quiet, to listen for the guiding voice within can bring about such a drastic change in one's life as to become almost unbelievable.

Edgar Cayce, America's foremost clairvoyant, found divine guidance for meditation while in a trancelike state of mind. Cayce passed this guidance on to all who will take the time to learn to meditate and, in turn, listen. The Cayce readings not only tell us how to meditate, but why and what to expect once we begin to put this age-old gentle art into practice each day.

Through the practice of meditation we can learn to savor life to its fullest. We learn that we are never alone, that help is always near. We begin intuitively to know whether the decisions we make are right or not. We can see illnesses fading by the wayside. We learn to give others a helping hand, to accept help from others. Cayce told us, "We readily see how, then, *in* meditation . . . that *healing* of *every* kind and nature may be disseminated on the wings of thought."

WHAT IS MEDITATION?

According to Edgar Cayce, "It is not musing, not daydreaming; but as ye find your bodies made of the physical, mental, and spiritual, it is attuning of the mental body and the physical body to its spiritual source.

"Then, it is the attuning of thy physical and mental attributes seeking to know the relationships to the Maker. THAT is true meditation.

"For, ye must learn to meditate—just as ye have learned to walk, to talk, to do any of the physical attributes of thy mind as compared to the relationships with the facts, the attitudes, the conditions, the environs of thy daily surroundings.

"Then, there must be a conscious contact with that which is a part of thy body-physical, thy body-mental, to thy soul-body or thy superconsciousness. The names indicate that ye have given it metes and bounds, while the soul is boundless—and is represented by many means or measures or manners in the expressions in the minds of each of you." (281-41)

Meditation is the tuning in to the God-consciousness in oneself. Meditation is the shutting out for a given period of time each day the many things which make a constant demand of everyone. It is the stilling of the mind to the hue and cry of the everyday world. It is the hearing of God's answers to our prayers. It is the awakening of a part of us which has lain dormant for a long, long time.

During meditation the seven spiritual centers of the body are opened, allowing the kundalini flow to rise. The spiritual centers are the glands, or ducts, of the endocrine system—pituitary, pineal, thyroid/parathyroid, thymus, cells of Leydig (lyden), adrenals, and gonads. The kundalini is the creative flow of energy which starts in the gonads and rises to the pineal, spilling over into the pituitary, the master center. The spiritual centers will be covered more fully in Chapter V.

As can readily be understood, meditation is not a game, nor an activity to be entered into for the fun of it or for experimental purposes. Nor is meditation a concentrated thought which leads to self-hypnosis. True and deep meditation is the attainment of becoming one with God, if only for a split second in time. To enter meditation means to focus on God.

Do not be deceived; meditation is not as easy or as simple as many would have one believe. It will seem rather difficult to sit still in one position and close the mind to the outer world. One will find there are many things pressing in, demanding this time. And oddly enough, one may find it strangely difficult to spare even fifteen minutes daily for meditation. It is as if one is being tested by a power beyond the conscious control.

If one does persevere to the point where the body and mind have been mastered, meditation still may not be what one expects it to be.

Upon being asked, "Why is it that at times my meditation seems unsatisfactory?" Cayce replied, "For ye are still in the flesh. Why did He say 'Father, why hast thou forsaken me?' Even when the world was being overcome, the flesh continued to rebel; for 'When I *would* do good, evil is present with me—but, though I take wings and fly to the utmost parts of the heavens, Thou art there; though I make my bed in hell, Thou are there.' So, when doubt and fear come, close thine *senses* to the *material* things and LOSE thineself *in* Him. Not that ye shall not be joyous in the things that partake of the pleasures even of life; for so did He—but keep thine consciousness ever alert, ready and willing to be the channel that will make known His love, and *He* will speak with thee!" (281-3)

In the practice of meditation, then, one must realize that he is still of a physical nature, and as such must make allowances for the physical and mental beings. But the time will come when one will experience that split second of Oneness with the Creator, and nothing in the known world can ever compare with it. When this has once happened, one will find himself looking forward to the time set aside for meditation.

As with most things, meditation must be learned. One would not take a lesson or two on a violin and expect to play a concerto. The same reasoning must apply to meditation. One must consistently meditate, day after day, not just occasionally. Meditate even when it seems hopeless, for with practice the door will be opened.

But "First study to know what meditation is. As has been indicated: the relationships first of body, mind, soul; then as these are understood, the *natural* forces, the *natural* manners of meditation will become as a part of self." (308-3)

Part of the soul's quest is enlightenment for one's physical and mental bodies. Many individuals spend years, sometimes a lifetime, perhaps many lifetimes, following the path, seeking truth and light.

So many are attempting to find the answers to such questions as, "Who am I? Why am I here? Where did I come from? Where do I go from here?" At this time in history, many have turned from orthodox churches because satisfactory answers have not been forthcoming. The pattern of conformity has been set for some and they are finding it increasingly difficult to accept the traditions and answers which have been handed down from their forefathers. Because one turns from something which has been acceptable for two thousand years does not necessarily indicate that he does not want to know the answers, or that he has stopped seeking.

Look within, the answers are there! Can you imagine the glorious feeling which must come when one knows that Christ has smiled upon one? That He has stood beside one and raised His hand in blessing? It is a happening that each one must experience for himself to fully appreciate and understand. When it does happen, one will know for a certainty that it is not his imagination. There is a vast difference between what can happen in meditation and the imagination playing tricks.

As has been said, there are many people asking questions of a spiritual nature at this time. Also, "There are others that care not whether there be such things as meditation, but depend upon someone else to do their thinking, or are satisfied to allow circumstances to take its course—and hope that sometime, somewhere, conditions and circumstances will adjust themselves to such a way that the best that may be will be their lot.

"Yet, to most of you, there must be something else— some desire, something that has prompted you in one manner or another to seek to be here now, that you may gather from a word, from an act, that will either give thee hope or make thee better satisfied with thy present lot, or to JUSTIFY thee in the course ye now pursue." (281-41)

To those who are questioning and seeking answers, meditation is the safest and most natural path to follow.

Until recent years, meditation was not widely accepted and practiced in the Western world. Many people were of the opinion that meditation belonged to the world of fanaticism and mysticism. There are still individuals who think that meditating means that one must sit and contemplate his navel for hours on end. Also, meditation, in the minds of many, has long been associated with Far Eastern religious philosophies.

The truth is far from these imaginings. The great Christian thinkers and philosophers of the Western world have practiced meditation for untold hundreds of years. And meditation is referred to throughout the Bible. It is safe to assume that Jesus, the Christ, meditated during His forty days and forty nights in the wilderness. He certainly did not pace up and down, wondering if He was doing the right thing. He went to the source of all knowledge, the Father within. And He is within each and every one of us if we will only take the time to listen for His voice.

In the practice of meditation, one must accept into his life the existence of a Supreme Power. It matters not what It is called—God, Buddha, Yahweh, or anyone of a dozen different names. Without the realization of a Creative Power, there would not be any voice to listen to, nothing to look forward to. One might as well be one of the lower forms of life, rather than the highest form of intelligence on the material plane.

In acknowledging a Supreme Power in one's life, one must also accept the existence of the Soul.

"Many say that ye have no consciousness of having a soul—yet the very fact that ye hope, that ye have a desire for better things, the very fact that ye are able to be sorry or glad, indicates an activity that takes hold upon something that is not temporal in its nature—something that passeth not away with the last breath that is drawn but that takes hold upon the very sources of its beginning—the SOUL—that which was made in the image of thy

Maker—not thy body, no—not thy mind, but thy SOUL was in the image of thy Creator." (281-41)

If Edgar Cayce was right in his psychic readings, and time and science have proved him correct time and time again, he confirmed that everyone has a soul and that they were created in the image of the Maker.

If one accepts the existence of the soul, one can also accept the fact the Creator of those souls would not permit them to exist without some means of communicating with Him. It is through meditation that one is able to establish this communication with Him.

Also, "Meditation is emptying self of all that hinders from the creative forces [kundalini] rising along the natural channels of the physical man to be disseminated through those centers [ductless glands] and sources that create the activities of the physical, the mental, the spiritual man; properly done must make one *stronger* mentally, physically, for has it not been given He went in the strength of that meat received for many days? Was it not given by Him who has shown us the Way, 'I have had meat that ye know not of?' And as we give out, so does the whole of man physically and mentally—become depleted, yet entering into the silence, entering into the silence in meditation, with a clean hand, a clean body, a clean mind, we may receive that strength and power that fits each individual, each soul, for a greater activity in this material world." (281-13)

Thus, one may see that meditation is also a cleansing process, a rejuvenation as it were, for the mental, physical, and spiritual bodies. In meditation, the creative forces move gradually upward from gland to gland, literally forming a figure eight in its upward and backward movement, cleansing and strengthening as it flows.

The consistent practice of meditation has been found to have wondrous effects upon individuals. For example, a number of alcoholics have found their inner strength and answers to haunting questions through the practice of meditation. This is not to say that they can continue drinking but rather that they no longer have the driving urge for alcohol. It has also recently been discovered that meditation is frequently the path back for many drug addicts. However, it is not advisable to go into deep meditation while on drugs as there can be certain negative forces attracted to some individuals, as we shall see in a later chapter which will deal with that element of meditation.

Meditation goes hand-in-hand with self-development not only for the mind, but for the physical body as well. Meditation is also the means of selfless development; of learning to let oneself be used as a channel of love and help for others.

"Hence as ye meditate, as ye analyze thyself—it isn't that there is to be given of the means so much, as it is to assist and aid others that ye meet day by day to analyze themselves—that they keep away from hate, animosity, jealousies, fears; those things that produce disturbing forces in the lives of thy neighbor, of thy friend, of thy people. Admonish them as He of old, that they walk in the ways that are in keeping with those things in which the Creative Forces of God are active, or are taken into the activities of the relationships day by day." (1315-10)

As each individual learns to know himself he is then

able to assist and help others onto the right path. Gradually one begins to understand that helping others is a twofold blessing, that one actually can climb to heaven on the arm of the brother he has helped. In aiding others, the Law of Love clarifies itself in the minds of many individuals.

The deeper spiritual purpose of meditation is the soul's attunement with its Creator. To help in the accomplishment of this desire, meditation should be approached in a spirit of love. It is this love which helps to break the barriers which have separated the soul from the One in whose image it was created. In turning within, rather than seeking answers from the outside, one eventually becomes aware of the Christ Consciousness within. And, ". . . the Christ Consciousness is the awareness within each soul, imprinted in pattern on the mind and waiting to be awakened by the will, of the soul's oneness with God." (5749-14)

Jesus and the Christ Consciousness are not to be confused. For "The Christ Consciousness is a univeral consciousness of the Father Spirit. The Jesus consciousness is that man builds as body worship." (5749-4)

In reaching a state of awareness in meditation, one is frequently aware of white light, which is symbolic of the Christ Consciousness. This rarely happens overnight but will take time and body and mental discipline. There will be times when the light is a tiny point of brilliant white, a mere pinpoint. And then there will be other times when the light is all-enveloping, with a shining warmth beyond anything the individual has ever known.

A reading pertaining to the light says, "Hence as one

reads or sees the interpretations of these in the life of Jesus of Nazareth, who became the Christ, the Savior, through fulfilling those purposes, one realizes that indeed He has become the Way, the Truth and the light.

"Thus the individual entity finds that the body, or that first creation of God, the mind, is the way; or the way through which light may come to the entity of the Father. For, as are the pronouncements in the law by Moses, 'To-day there is set before thee good and evil, life and death. And say not who will descend from heaven to bring a message, or who may come from over the sea, for Lo, it is within thine own heart.'

"And how well this is completed in that promise, that pronouncement, that admonition given by Him as He led the way to fulfill in the garden and on the Cross the law itself,—to demonstrate that separation from God might indeed be broken away forever. As He Gave, 'In my Father's house are many mansions; if it were not so I would have told you. I go to prepare a place, that where I am, there you may be also.'

"Thus, we see the relationship each soul bears to the Father, as to the way, the Christ,—by wholly trusting in Him day by day. As He said, 'I stand continually at the door of thy heart. Open and I will enter.'

"How do ye open? Through searching, seeking, humbling thyself before the throne of grace and mercy, as was manifested in Him; acknowledging Him as thy Lord, thy Master, yea thy Elder Brother.

"He has also given, 'If ye open I will come and abide with thee.'

"This, then, is the manner, the way, the truth, the

light, through which this entity may find its true relationships to the Creative Forces." (2845-1)

He, then, is the light. And that which is sought in meditation. Becoming aware of the light is a spontaneous happening and the glorious sensation of once having experienced it causes one to work consistently for the experience. The soul recognizes the light as its source of beginning. In the white light one knows he is reunited with his Creator. In the Book of John, 8:12, it is written, "Thus spake Jesus again unto them, saying, I am the Light of the world: he that followeth me shall not walk in Darkness, but shall have the Light of Life."

The white light is described by the Mundaka Upanishad as, "This is the light of light; when it shines, the sun does not shine." There is no light to be compared with the one which is sought in meditation. The whitest of whites, it is composed of all the colors in the spectrum which are visible to the physical eye, and perhaps the many unseen colors which one is told exist but cannot be seen by the human eye under ordinary conditions.

There is a shining radiance to the light which might be compared to the one encountered by Paul on the road to Damascus. Or, as Edgar Cayce said, "He, that Christ Consciousness, is that first spoken of in the beginning when God said, 'Let there be light, and there was light.' And that is the light manifested in the Christ." (2879-1)

THE DIFFERENCE BETWEEN MEDITATION AND PRAYER

There is a vast difference between meditation and prayer. Prayer is the lower self petitioning the higher self for spiritual guidance. In prayer one talks to God, in meditation one listens for the answers of God. During meditation one learns to listen for the still, small voice within.

In analyzing the difference between prayer and meditation, Cayce said, "As it has been defined or given in an illustrated manner by the Great Teacher, prayer is the *making* of one's conscious self more in attune with the spiritual forces that may manifest in a material world, and is *ordinarily* given as a *cooperative* experience of *many* individuals when all are asked to come in one accord . . .

". . . That which may be the pouring out of the personality of the individual, or a group who enter in for the purpose of either outward show to be seen by men; or that enter in even as in the closet of one's inner self and pours out self that the inner man may be filled with the spirit of the Father in His merciful kindness to men.

"Now draw the comparisons for meditation: Meditation, then, is prayer, but is prayer from *within* the *inner* self, and partakes not only of the physical inner man but the soul that is aroused by the spirit of man from within." (281-13)

When one prays, that one is making an effort to communicate with the Creator. One is asking for direction, for understanding, for attunement. Meditation is listening to the Divine within.

Many individuals wonder, "Is it correct when thinking of God to think of God as impersonal force or energy, everywhere present; or as an intelligent listening mind, which is aware of every individual on earth and who intimately knows everyone's needs and how to meet them?"

The answer is, "Both! For He is also the energies in the finite moving in material manifestation. He is also the Infinite, with the awareness. And thus as ye attune thy own consciousness, thy own awareness, the unfoldment of the presence within beareth witness with the presence without. And as the Son gave, 'I and my Father are one,' then *ye* come to know that ye and the Father are one, that ye abide in Him.

"Thus we find the manifestations of life, the manifestations of energy, the manifestations of power and MOVES in material, are the representations of the manifestation of the Infinite God.

"Yet as we look into the infinity of space and time we realize there is then that force, that influence also that is aware of the needs, and there is also that will, that choice given to the souls of men that they may be used, that they may be one, that they may apply same in their own feeble, weak ways perhaps; yet that comes to mean, comes to signify, comes to manifest in the lives of those that have lost their way, that very influence ye seek in the knowledge of God.

"For until ye become a savior, as a help to some soul that has lost hope, lost its way, ye do not fully comprehend the God within, the God without." (1158-14)

Earlier it was mentioned that selfless development is a large part of meditation. One cannot fully understand the God within and the God without until he has learned to understand and help his fellow man. Nor does one understand the meaning of prayer until that prayer becomes a self-less one. This is not meant to imply that one does not pray for himself, but rather that it should not be in a selfish manner.

Prayer does not take the place of meditation, or vice versa. Prayer is the means of making known to the Father that one has recognized his needs and the needs of others. Prayer is the voicing, whether aloud or silently, of those recognitions. The needs may be mental, physical, or spiritual. And until one is aware of the things which are lacking, if they were given to him, he would not know them.

Prayer, then, is a supplication to God. In meditation the prayer is rewarded by the answering of the still small voice of the Christ Consciousness within. For, "He has promised if ye call, I will be there."

". . . set definite periods for prayer; set definite periods for meditation. Know the difference between each. Prayer, in short is appealing to the divine from within self, the divine without self, and meditation is keeping still in body, in mind, in heart, listening, to the voice of thy Maker." (5368-1)

SELECTED PRAYERS FROM THE CAYCE READINGS

"Father, may there be in me that mind, that desire, which prompted the living of the life of Thy Son in this material world.

"May I be drawn nearer and nearer to that understanding of the purposes of the manifestations of life, making my will one with Thy will, feeling and realizing Thy presence abiding day by day in my every experience;

realizing life's activities are the manifestations of Thy love. Keep me in the right way." (282-6)

"Father, God, Thou art life! Thou art hope! Thou art justice! Thou art mercy! In these may I, Thy servant, claim Thy care, Thy love; that my body may be cleansed as my mind is cleansed, that I may be before Thee holy and acceptable unto Thee to do service to my fellow man in *Thy* name; and that the glory of Thy love as manifested in the Christ, my Savior, our Savior, may be manifested more and more in the earth." (370-5)

"As I open my heart, my mind to Thee, O God, with the joyousness of the new experiences that may be mine, wilt Thou be the guide. May I make my will, my mind, my soul, daily in accord with that service that Thou wouldst have me render to my fellow man. Let the words of my mouth and the meditations of my heart be more and more acceptable unto Thee, my Lord and redeemer. For Thou may live in me as Thou hast promised, that the *glory* of the Father may be manifested in those that love His ways. Help Thou mine unbelief. Make Thou mine heart clean, renewing a righteous spirit within me, for Thou hast promised to be near." (557-3)

Chapter II

AIDS TO MEDITATION

A period of fifteen minutes is a good starting point for those who are just beginning to meditate. This may not seem like a very long period of time; but it is much better to slowly discipline the body and mind, getting them accustomed to a short period of absolute stillness and silence and then gradually increase the length of time until the desired period is reached.

In Richard Wilhelm's translation of *The Secret of the Golden Flower*, it is written, "Children, take heed! If for a day you do not practice meditation, this light streams out, who knows whither? If you only meditate for a quarter of an hour, by it you can do away with the ten thousand aeons and a thousand births."

The metabolism, which releases energy for the physical body, operates differently for everyone. There are morning people and there are night people, which means that each individual must find the time of day or night which is best suited to his body and disposition for meditation. "The better period would be that which will be set as a period in which the body and mind may be dedicated to that. Then keep your promise to self, and to your inner self, and to your Maker, or that to which ye dedicate thy body, mind and soul." (2982-3)

Once the time has been established which is most conducive to meditation, do not set this as rote, or in a grudging manner, but rather as the time when heart and mind will be happy at the prospect of entering the Silence. Meditation should become the time of the daily routine most looked forward to.

Inner peace will be one of the first rewards of meditation. Individuals will begin to find that if the mind be stormy with the petty problems of everyday living, it will begin to emerge from meditation with the freshness of a newly rain-washed sky.

It is not always easy for those of a Western-oriented mind to learn to discipline the physical and mental bodies for meditation. However, "If the success is not found in the first, then seek again and again *at the same period* (that may be chosen); either early in the morning or in the noonday or in the evening, whenever chosen to give that time to *His* making aware in thee that thou shouldst do.

"For, He has ever promised; and He is faithful to those that cry out unto Him in the night or in the day. For, He will not leave thy soul desolate; neither will He allow thee to be burdened beyond that thou art able to bear. But he whom the Lord loveth, He purgeth everyone; that each soul may be the purer, in the light." (412-7)

In the aeons that the soul has been apart from its Creator, the bodies which it has inhabited have repeatedly adjusted themselves to the many demands made upon them in their struggle for survival in an ever increasingly competive world. Individuals have learned to pamper the physical bodies, but rare is the time which is set aside for the soul. Since the soul was created in the image of its Maker, isn't it logical to assume that it would yearn for a re-union? When one enters into meditation he is granting the desire of the soul to communicate with its Creator.

"In the material world we find a set time, a period, for the accomplishing of, for the carrying out of, the daily tasks that may add to the betterment of a commercial association in any given field.

"We see definite periods set aside for the replenishing of the body with the fuels that may be consumed and assimilated by the body.

"Foods of the spirit are as necessary to the mental well being as the carnal forces of food for the maintaining of an equilibrium in the physical body.

"Hence, set a portion of self to those periods of communing with the inner self through meditation and prayer to the Giver of all good and perfect gifts; knowing there is a mediator that ever stands ready to make intercession, and He has given those promises that anywhere, any time that the soul calls, He will harken, He *will* guide."
(274-3)

MATERIAL AIDS

Each individual reacts to different stimuli in a different manner. The aid which might enable one person to go into meditation could very well have the opposite effect upon another. Personally, I seem to have the compulsion to wash my feet before I prepare to meet my God. To me, this seems to be a symbolic cleansing of the whole body. Perhaps the origin of this simple act lies buried within the memory of another lifetime.

Also, the gentle sound of a Tibetan temple bell brings my body to a rigidly upright position and I feel as if I am soaring away to another dimension. The first time I heard such a bell tears streamed down my face and I felt a deep sadness for which I had no explanation. Perhaps the sound struck a vibratory pattern hidden deep within the soul-memory and for an instant it returned to a long-ago day.

The various aids employed by different individuals in creating an atmosphere conducive to meditation should remain aids and nothing more. For, ". . . know that these are but those things that will make for the arousing of the *inner* self, and *not* the force that arises; rather a material element for the producing of same." (355-1)

In discussing meditation, one individual asked, "Should I carry these stones on my person? And how may I know through meditation the message they would give?"

The reply applies to all who seek. "If necessary. And how may ye know? These do not give the message! Listen to no message of a stone, of a number, even of a star; for they are but servants of the Lord and Master of all—even as thou!" (707-2)

The different aids tend to lend assurances to the physical mind and, as in the case of the Tibetan temple bell, perhaps trigger a memory pattern which could very well help in the unraveling of a present-day problem. Each individual must find that which is best suited for him, whether it be a temple bell, a stone, or what have you.

One individual who apparently vibrated to things of an oriental nature, was told in a Cayce reading, "And it is well that self, when contemplating and meditating, surround self with the environs of an oriental nature; for the dress itself should ever be rather the robes or loose clothing about the body. There should ever be something that bespeaks either of the scarab, bull or serpent; with the perfumes of the East." (355-1)

Experience and intuition will tell each individual that which is best for him.

Music is also quite helpful in setting the atmosphere for meditation. The choice of the music is entirely up to the individual. Needless to say, it should be soft and soothing. And it should be turned off before actually going into meditation.

If an individual feels it will benefit him, help him grow in awareness, to create an atmosphere that is familiar by surrounding himself with objects of a certain nature, then by all means do so. But remember:

". . . these are but lights, but signs in thine experience, they are but as a candle that one stumbles not in the dark. But worship *not* the light of the candle; rather that to which it may guide thee in thy service. So, whether from the vibrations of numbers, of metals, of stones, these are merely to become the necessary influences to make thee in attune, one with the Creative Forces; just as the pitch of a song of praise is not the song nor the message therein, but is a helpmeet for those who would find strength in the service of the Lord. So, use them to attune self. How, ye ask? As ye apply, ye are given the next step." (707-2)

HEAD AND NECK EXERCISES

A great deal of life's daily tension becomes concentrated in the neck and shoulders, resulting in muscular knots and aches. To enter into a state of meditation, it is necessary to let the body utterly relax, allowing tension to flow out. The following exercises have a tendency to relax the body and align the spine, allowing the creative energy to flow more freely throughout the body.

Sit upright, *spine erect*, with the feet planted firmly on the floor.

Do each of the following exercises three times.

Lean the head forward to the chest and bring it back to the normal position.

Lean the head backward as far as it will go and bring it back to the normal position.

Lean the head to the left shoulder and bring it back to the normal position.

Lean the head to the right shoulder and bring it back to the normal position.

Lean the head to the chest and rotate it in a wide circle, counter-clockwise, ending at the chest. Bring it back to the normal position.

Lean the head to the chest and rotate it in a wide

circle, clockwise, ending at the chest. Bring it back to the normal position.

Repeat each set of exercises three times before going on to the next set. Do each in a slow, deliberate manner, allowing the body to benefit from each one. The exercises become meaningless if they are hurried through or treated in a manner whereby one acts as if they are a thing to be done and finished with. Occasionally, stiffness may result in the neck and shoulders when the exercises are first started, but it soon passes.

The exercises help to put the body in a quiet mood. When first learning to meditate, it is more difficult to sit perfectly still for fifteen minutes than one might expect. The body, of its own volition, will itch and demand to be scratched with the hands automatically answering the call. Also, there will probably be involuntary muscular movements and twitchings. These and perhaps other unthinking movements will take place in the body. One must teach the body that the calls for attention will not always be answered. Eventually the body itchings and twitchings will learn that it is of no use and stop. Until that does happen, it must remain a conscious effort to ignore the attempts of the physical body to gain attention.

With dedicated practice, it will not take too long for one to become completely unaware of the body during meditation. To all intents and purposes, it will simply cease to exist. Finally the point will be reached where, if suddenly called upon to make a physical move during meditation, one will know he has arms and hands, legs and feet, but for a bit one will wonder where they are. It will take a conscious effort to make them behave as they should. When this point is reached, one can truly say the physical body is under control.

BREATHING EXERCISES

Following the physical exercises, there are certain breathing exercises which help in the preparation for meditation.

"In breathing," states a Cayce reading, "take into the right nostril, STRENGTH! Exhale through thy mouth. Intake in thy left nostril, exhaling through the right; opening the centers of thy body—if it is first prepared to thine *own* understanding, thine *own* concept of what *ye* would have if ye would have a visitor, if ye would have a companion, if ye would have thy bridegroom." (281-28)

The breathing exercises, then, are helpful in the opening of the centers of the body, which are the seven glands referred to as the seven spiritual centers.

The following breathing exercises are from the Cayce readings. Each one should be done three times. Each time, breathe deeply, hold the air in the lungs for a bit, exhale slowly and deliberately.

Inhale through the right nostril and exhale through the mouth. (You may have to hold the left nostril closed by placing the finger along side it.)

Inhale through the left nostril and exhale through the right nostril, keeping the mouth closed thereby letting the air pass down into the lungs and cross over as it returns to be exhaled.

As has been pointed out, the breathing exercises have a direct effect upon the spiritual centers of the body. The breathing exercises and its effects are described thus: ". . . in the body there is that center in which the soul is expressive, creative in its nature,—the Leydig center.

"By this breathing, this may be made to expand—as it moves along the path that is taken in its first inception, at conception, and opens the seven centers of the body that radiate or are active upon the organisms of the body.

"As this life force is expanded, it moves first from the Leydig center through the adrenals, in what may be termed an upward trend, to the pineal and to the centers in control of the emotions—or reflexes through the nerve forces of the body.

"Thus an entity puts itself, through such an activity, into association or in conjunction with all it has EVER been or may be. For it loosens the physical consciousness to the universal consciousness." (2457-1)

As one can understand, the breathing exercises tend to be instrumental in causing the life forces or creative energies to commence moving in an upward flow, from center to center, finally arriving at the pituitary, or the "third eye" as it is sometimes called.

In realizing the part which is played by the physical and the breathing exercises in meditation, one better begins to realize how every part of the body is tied to the whole. And the care of the body in every way is of utmost importance.

"There is the body-physical—with all its attributes for the functioning of the body in a three-dimensional or a manifested earth plane.

"Also there is the body-mental—which is that directing influence of the physical, the mental and the spiritual emotions and manifestations of the body; or the way, the manner in which conduct is related to self, to individuals, as well as to things, conditions, and circumstances. While the mind may not be seen by the physical senses, it can be sensed by others; that is, others may sense the conclusions that have been drawn by the body-mind of an individual, by the manner in which such an individual conducts himself in relationship to things, conditions or people.

"Then there is the body-spiritual or soul-body—that eternal something that is invisible. It is only visible to that consciousness in which the individual entity in patience becomes aware of its relationship to the mental and physical being.

"All of these then are one—in an entity; just as it is considered, realized or acknowledged that the body, mind and soul are one,—that God, the Son and the Holy Spirit are one.

"Then in the physical body there ARE those influences, then, through which each of these phases of an entity may or does become an active influence.

"There may be brought about an awareness of this by the exercising of the mind, through the manner of directing the breathing." (2475-1)

POSTURE

After the physical and the breathing exercises, one assumes the posture which will be maintained during the period of meditation. To some, there may be confusion as to which is the best position. The answer applies to all who ask.

"As has been given, there are given to each their own respective manners, from their varied experiences, as to *how*, as to form. If form [posture] becomes that that is the guiding element, then the hope or faith is lost in form." (262-17)

It matters not, then, which is the position that is selected so long as it is comfortable and not distracting to the mind during meditation.

The position assumed can be that of the lotus, with the hands cupped in the manner of the lotus blossom. Or it can be the position of the American Indian of sitting on the heels. There are some individuals who prefer to sit upright in a straight-back chair, with the feet planted firmly on the floor.

If lying flat on the back in bed or on the floor is the most comfortable, then do that. However, in the lying down position, always "crossing the hands over the solar plexus, either on the plexus area—the 9th dorsal—or the umbilici [the navel]." (440-8) If this is not done, there can come about "an unbalancing of the forces through which, in the physical body, the psychic forces are opened." (440-8) This unbalancing will be covered in a later chapter.

The most important thing to be remembered, regardless of the position selected, is that it is *always of paramount importance that the spine be as straight as possible*, allowing the creative energy to flow upward from center to center.

CHANTING

Some individuals may find that certain chants will be helpful in raising the personal vibrations prior to entering into the Silence. For some, chanting will prove too much of a distraction and should not be used.

A chant from the readings which is frequently used goes thus: Ar-ar-r-r-r-e-e-e-o-o-o-m-m-m.

". . . as ye begin with the incantation of the Ar-ar-r-r-r —the e-e-e, the o-o-o, the m-m-m, *raise* these in thyself; and ye become close in the presence of thy Maker—as is *shown* in thyself! They that do such for selfish motives do so to their own undoing. Thus has it oft been said, the fear of the Lord is the beginning of wisdom." (281-28)

Individuals who are drawn to things of an oriental nature, including incense, may very well find the following chant to be beneficial in the practice of meditation.

"Begin with that which is oriental in its nature—oriental incense. Let the mind become, as it were, attuned to such by the humming, producing those sounds of O-O-O-ah-ah-umm-o-o-o; not as to become monotonous, but 'feel' the essence of the incense through the body forces in its motion of body. This will open the kundalini [creative] forces of the body. Then direct same to be a blessing to others. These arise from the creative center of the body itself, and as they move through the various centers direct same; else they may become more disturbing than helpful. Surround self ever with that pur-

pose, 'Not my will, O God, but Thine be done, ever'—
and the entity will gain vision, perception, and—most of
all—judgment." (2823-3)

By trial and error, step by step, one finds that which
is best suited to help him enter into meditation. One experiments with various aids, discarding each as he finds
he no longer needs it. One learns not to let the aids lend
confusion, nor does one ever become totally dependent
upon them.

As well as learning the different aids and forms which
may prove beneficial to meditation, one should also,
"Study day by day to show self approved unto God
through the applications in the daily associations with
man, the fruits of the spirit; as, making the activities in
keeping with, 'As ye would that men should do unto you,
do ye even unto them.' Patience, persistence, loving-kind-
ness, love, graciousness, soft words rather than anger;
these will make for the abilities of the mental forces to
divide correctly the words of truth that may be received
in the periods of meditation when there may be the
attuning of self to those influences in the spiritual realm.
Yet on each occasion so guard self as to bar the evil
influences, by surrounding self with the love of the Master, of the Christ Consciousness. And, in this manner may
there be opened for the body-consciousness, for the physical-mental abilities, the proper relations, the proper activities of the body in the developing of the soul and
spiritual influences of the entity, the soul." (412-7)

Chapter III

BODY, MIND, AND SOUL

CLEANSING

A dispelling of the barriers which separates one from the Christ Consciousness within is one of the first steps one must take before he may hope to reach the ultimate goal. The mental attitude with which one enters the Silence must be cleansed of all that would hinder progress.

There are a number of ways this cleansing may take place. For example, examine the everyday activities. Does the wrong kind of activity, such as films, television, certain kinds of music, and things of that nature tend to plant thoughts in the mind which have a way of building stumbling blocks? By no means am I suggesting that these particular activities be abstained from, but I am suggesting that individuals choose things which will be steppingstones for the building and cleansing of the mind and body.

Prayer is a very important means of cleansing the mental and spiritual bodies. Before the offering of love can be laid at the feet of the Master, it must first be offered to one's fellow man. The brief prayer of "Lord, he is Thine, even as I am Thine. Do that which will bring about peace and harmony between us," helps to cleanse the mind of ill feelings toward another. It also serves to remind individuals that it is not only others who offend, but oneself as well. The gift of forgiving others and ourselves is one of the greatest of all gifts.

". . . In thine experience, have you ever found that to 'get even' with anyone made thee happy? To forgive them is divine and brings Happiness to all. *These* things sow in the lives, in the hearts, in the minds of others 'Grace and mercy, Lord, not sacrifice, not judgment.'" (262-109)

A clean body and clean surroundings are also to be taken into consideration in the practice of meditation.

"In whatever manner that to thine own consciousness is a cleansing of the body and the mind, that ye may present thyself CLEAN before thyself and before thy God, DO! Whether washing of the body with water, purging of same with oils, or surrounding same with music or incense. But DO THAT THY CONSCIOUSNESS directs thee! No questioning! For he that doubteth has already built his barrier." (826-11)

As has been mentioned, in the practice of meditation, the spiritual centers are opened. By the opening of these special glands in the physical body, in the rise and flow of the creative energy, a spiritual cleansing process takes place. This particular cleansing helps to remove some of the stumbling blocks which have separated individuals from the Christ Consciousness within.

The spiritual cleansing helps to rid one of hates, fears, angers, frustrations, and the ego trips which many individuals are subject to in their existence in a material world.

"First, *cleanse* the room; cleanse the body; cleanse the surroundings, in thought, in act! Approach not the inner man, or the inner self, with a grudge or an unkind thought held against *any* man or do so to thine own undoing sooner or later." (281-13)

FAITH

The promise upon which a successful meditation is built is *Faith*. The Faith that He will answer when we call. It doesn't seem reasonable to think that the call will be answered if a negative or doubtful attitude is taken. The following reading shows very clearly how one may build a Christ-like faith within himself.

". . . If the entity will read or study or analyze how the Master treated children, young people, during His ministry in the earth, it will be seen how oft He used children, the young people, as the hope of the world, as to how unless each individual puts away those selfish desires which arise and become as little children, one may never quite understand the simplicity of Christ's faith;

Christ-like faith,
Christ-like simplicity,

Christ-like forgiveness,
Christ-like love,
Christ-like helpfulness to others." (1223-9)

In observing the deep and simple faith that little children have, in the trusting love they have for others, one can better begin to understand the meaning of the words *faith* and *trust*.

Faith, it would seem, is the interpretation of "Unless ye become as little children, ye cannot enter into the kingdom of heaven." While one is a living, physical being, the most of heaven that one can know lies within, in the coming to know the Christ Consciousness.

KARMA

There is scarcely an individual who, at one time or another, has not wondered about the seeming injustice of life. Nearly everyone asks, "Why did this, that, or the other, happen to so-and-so? What did he (or I) ever do to deserve that?" Sometimes excuses or reasons can be very easily found; at other times, the logic of what has happened escapes all reasoning.

The word *karma* is a very old word, originating in the Far East. And it is referred to at different times throughout the Cayce readings. Karma involves the law of "cause and effect," or, for every cause there is an effect. Karma, as related to individuals, is frequently the reason why certain things happen to some people and not to others.

"Well that karma be understood, and how it is to be met. For, in various thought—whether considered philosophy or religion, or whether from the more scientific manner of cause and effect—karma is all of these and more. Rather it may be likened unto a piece of food, whether fish or bread, taken into the system; it is assimilated by the organs of digestion, and then those elements that are gathered from same are made into forces that flow through the body, giving the strength and vitality to an animate object, or being, or body. So, in experiences of a soul, in a body, in an experience in the earth. Its thoughts make for that upon which the soul feeds, as do the activities that are carried on from the thought of the period make for the ability of retaining or maintaining the active or active principle of the thought through an experience. Then, the soul re-entering into a body under a different environ either makes for the expanding of that it has made *through* the experiences in the sojourn in a form that is called in some religions as destiny of the soul, in another philosophy that which has been builded must be met in some way or manner, or in the more scientific manner that a certain cause produces a certain effect. Hence we see that karma is *all* of these and more. What more? Ever since the entering of spirit and soul into matter there has been a way of redemption for the soul, to make an association and connection with the Creator, *through* the love *for* the Creator that is in its experience. Hence, this, too, must be taken into consideration; that karma may mean development *for self*—and must be met in that way or manner, or it may mean that which has been acted upon by the cleansing influences of the way and manner through which the soul, the mind-soul, or the soul-mind is purified, or purifies itself, and hence those changes come about—and some people term it 'Lady Luck' or 'the body is born under a lucky star.' It's what the soul-mind has done *about* the source of redemption of the soul! Or it may be yet that of cause and effect, as related to the soul, the mind, the spirit, the body." (440-5)

Thus it is that the karmic patterns are imprinted upon each soul as it moves through lifetime after lifetime. At some point or other, the soul in its quest for perfection in returning to its Creator meets each and every thing that it has been involved with at some other time. Every deed (cause) must have its payment (effect). This includes the good things as well as the others.

It is during meditation that one is sometimes made aware of things which might have happened aeons ago. In the cells of the adrenal glands (one of the seven spiritual centers), it is believed that the karmic memories are stored. Since we have already learned that these centers become active during meditation, we now know how it is possible that one may be made aware of certain things which would otherwise not have been known to one. This is related to the cleansing process which takes place in the physical, mental, and spiritual bodies during meditation.

VIBRATIONS

In each individual, vibrations play a vital part in the raising of the Christ Consciousness which is within. It is through certain vibrations that each is able to raise the creative energy flow.

"All force is vibration, as all comes from one central vibration and its activity into, out from, and its own creative forces, as given, with that of the divine as manifested in man, is [the] same vibration—taking form. Here, we may give a dissertation . . . as to what Creative Energy is, as related to man and his activity, and as the forces as are seen in and about man . . . true it was said, 'Come let us make man in our own image,' in His own image created God, or created by God, was man. Then containing all of the vibrations that were without, were given into that whole being of man—which in *its* vibrations gave man the soul. *Above* all else created, see? Then we see how the evolution of force in vibration brought up to the point wherein man becomes one *with* the Creative Energy, or the God-head—with the ability to become that that he is *not* at the beginning, by making himself absent from the will of the Creator or Creative Energy. How? In that the ability to create mentally, and with the hand *makes* that which IS the created force of that mind, and with that may make destructive forces for self. Hence man becomes one *with* the Creative Energy, or away *from* that Creative Energy. When man makes himself one *with*—then all things were created by him, without him there was nothing created that was created, or made—and are then *his* by rightful heir, even as shown in His Son, wherein man shown the way, or the access to this all Creative Energy." (900-422)

Thus we see that it is through vibrations that man

came into being. Through the vibrations raised in meditation, man may become whatever it is that he desires. During meditation, vibrations of a spiritual nature are brought into being, and man may return to the Creative Energy, from whence he came, or not; it is as man chooses.

Everything, whether it be a chair, the petal of a daisy, or man himself, is vibration. In every known thing there are vibrations of one kind or another. And they can be constructively or destructively used for man's good or otherwise.

As an example: "Each functioning organ of the sensory system reflects a different vibration to produce to the brain the functioning of the organs given to the body to express to the physical the action of that organ, that is the sense of taste, which is based both through the tongue and at the root of the tongue and is connected with the sensory organs and to the pneumogastric nerve, and to the brain three million times less than the vibration necessary to produce hearing or sight, that of speech being even three times greater than the sense of hearing or sight; that is the highest vibration we have in the body at all." (5681-1)

We are told, then, that speech carries the highest vibrations of all in the physical body. Thus is seen the power of the spoken word, or prayer.

It is not difficult to understand how the very thoughts which one might think would affect the vibrations of a body. The atmosphere one surrounds oneself with, the contacts in daily life, all of the things one would not ordinarily give a passing thought to, affect the vibrations of one's being. In the knowledge of vibrations and their effects upon one, it becomes clearer why cleanliness of the body and mind are so important to the practice of meditation.

It would be practically impossible for one to think and act in one manner and hope to become another way. The inner vibrations are reflected outward, as well as to the inner man. Therefore, as each thinks and speaks, so he becomes.

Chapter IV

IDEALS AND AFFIRMATIONS

Various things are achieved through the practice of meditation such as physical well being, peace of mind, self knowledge as well as other things which are dependent upon the individual meditating. However, the primary purpose of meditation should remain the same for everyone—self-less development to the Christ Consciousness within.

IDEALS

In attempting to open the door through which all peace comes, it becomes necessary to determine exactly what the spiritual, mental, and material (physical) ideals are. In ascertaining the different ideals: "First find deep within self that purpose, that ideal to which ye would attain. Make that ideal one with thy purpose in Him. Know that within thine own body, thine own temple, He —thy Lord, thy Master—has promised to meet thee. Then as ye turn within, meditate upon those promises from body-mind (which is the soul and the mental self, or the Father AND the Son in activity), so that there arises that consciousness of the at-onement with Him. And there may come—yea, there will come—those directions; by that constant communion with Him. USE this, practice this in thy daily dealings with thy fellow man; not as one that would make himself ABOVE his brothers, but even as the Master, who made Himself one WITH His brethren, that He might save the more." (2533-1)

As one studies that which is given to him to know, he gradually becomes more aware of the spiritual, mental, and material ideals. When the ideals have clarified themselves in the mind, do not just continue to think about them, but write them on paper.

"Do not, then, merely have a verbal or vocal ideal. Do write what is thy ideal. Begin with that under these three headings: Spiritual, Mental, Material [physical]." (3051-2)

The following table is an example of that used by the Association for Research and Enlightenment.

IDEALS

SPIRITUAL	MENTAL	MATERIAL
". . . thy spiritual concept of the ideal, whether it be Jesus, Buddha, mind, material, God, or whatever is the word which indicates to self the ideals spiritual."	". . . write the ideal mental attitude, as may arise from concepts of the spiritual, [in] relationship to self, to home, to friends, to neighbors, to thy enemies, to things, to conditions."	". . . the ideal material . . . Not of conditions, but what has brought, what does bring into manifestation the spiritual and mental ideals. What relationships does such bring to things, to individuals, to situations?"

"Then set about to apply the knowledge ye have attained . . . It's the application of same that counts." (5091-3)

"And write what is thine own ideal. As ye may find, these may change from time to time. For each soul grows in grace, in knowledge, in understanding. Just as the awareness, the unfoldments come to the self AS the entity applies that it has chosen and does choose from day to day." (3051-2)

As one uses the inner knowledge which has been made known to him, he changes and begins to grow in spiritual awareness. As the changes and developments take place, one may very well see that the ideals will also change. As the changes are noted, do not hesitate to change the ideals accordingly.

As one grows, there will be a tendency for the ideals no longer to be self-centered but they will begin to project out to one's fellow man. It is here that one may see the Christ Spirit manifested from day to day.

One will begin to consciously notice that changes are taking place in every fiber of one's being. The door has been knocked upon and, as He promised, it has been opened. Perhaps only a bit at first, but now the certain knowledge is there that it can be opened wide and the white light will begin to envelop one with His love and understanding.

AFFIRMATIONS

With the stilling of the mind and body, one begins to separate oneself from worldly things for the period of time chosen to meditate. As most individuals will have discovered, this is not exactly an easy accomplishment. The stilling of the physical body is relatively simple as compared to the stilling of the mind, or mental body. It is a natural experience for the mind to skip from thought to thought, very often bringing to the surface things which one might have believed buried and gone forever.

Focusing on a spiritual affirmation can be of tremendous help in quieting the mind and curbing its wanderings. Each time it is consciously realized that the mind has sidetracked itself and gone off on its own merry way, gently bring it back to the affirmation.

It is with care that the affirmation is selected. "For He stands ever at the door of thy conscience; He stands ever as a lamp to thy feet, as a light to the pathway. And unless ye shatter same by the greater material desire, He will lead the way." (849-17)

A spiritual affirmation is a building block for the individual using it and contributes to the growth toward that which is being affirmed.

As in the selection of aids which will help an individual to enter into meditation, the same individuality applies in the selection of an affirmation. ". . . as has been indicated—each soul, each entity should of its own volition and desire perfect that approach which to self answers that need within. No one may tell another how to fall in love, or how to bear up under same in meeting desire in self. Neither may one tell another that which answers to that awareness within." (2441-2)

The affirmation tends to help set the spiritual vibrations in motion, and for each individual these are different, just as the ideals are different for each one. As the spiritual centers begin to open, the affirmation also acts as an aid in preventing contact with undesired influences.

"Then as ye open in thy meditation, first surround self with the thought [affirmation], the prayer, the desires that Jesus, in His promises, guide thee in thy seeking.

"THEN ye have set yourself aright.

"Then again as ye raise thy power of vibratory forces through the body, ye give thyself in body, in mind, in purpose, in desire, into the hands, into the keeping of His purposes with thee." (853-9)

To enter into the Silence, the mind must be lifted to a higher level of thinking than it usually attains. while working with things of a material nature. The affirmations not only accomplish this, but they also help to trigger the memory pattern of the soul-body, thereby opening the path to the Divine within.

There are a number of excellent affirmations, including favorite Bible verses or Psalms. Following is a selection of spiritual affirmations from the Edgar Cayce readings.

"Not my way, Lord. Have Thine own way with me, that I may ever in this experience of every nature, of every kind be as a channel of blessings to those I contact day by day, in every way, in every manner." (657-3)

"I am Thine, Lord! In the love Thou hast shown through the Christ, bring to this body of mine that Thou seest, that Thou knowest is best; that I may be the more perfect manifestation of Thy love among the children of men!" (1363-1)

"May the desire of my heart be such that I may become more and more aware of the spirit of the Father, through the Christ, manifesting in me." (262-57)

"Let the knowledge of the Lord so permeate my being that there is less and less of self, more and more of God, in my dealings with my fellow man; that the Christ may be in all, through all, in His Name." (262-95)

LIGHT OF PROTECTION

As the spiritual affirmation begins to take form in the mind, visualize the physical body as it sits in its meditative position. Then, mentally surround it with a white light of protection. As will be shown in a later chapter, possession by undesired influences is a very real thing and the white light is protective in its nature.

The light of protection which mentally surrounds one during meditation is not to be confused with the symbolic white light of the Christ Consciousness.

However, visualizing the body surrounded by the protective light is tantamount to the protection of the Master. "So, in opening self—as should every soul (for the body is the temple of the soul, the temple of the spirit of the Father)—surround self with that which is ever present *with* the Father, and He is faithful; for He has given, 'As ye seek me, as ye ask in my name, that will be thine. For, as I go to the Father, and ye abide in me and I in the Father, the deeds that ye do in the body may be manifesting—and be examples of—the love of the Father to the sons of men.'" (276-6)

THE WHITE LIGHT

I realize that we have touched on the white light which is symbolic of the Christ Consciousness within, but to avoid confusion between the light of protection and the white light of meditation, it would seem that a few more words are in order.

The white light which is seen and felt in meditation cannot be fully visualized, nor can it be satisfactorily described to another. The white light is intangible, yet there is an awareness of solidity about it at the same time. And, strangely, the desire to speak about it to others is very often absent.

It is written in Isaiah 60:19, "The sun shall be no more thy light by day; neither for brightness shall the moon give light unto thee: but the Lord shall be unto thee an everlasting light, and thy God thy glory." Thus it is with the white light of meditation.

PRAYER

The difference between prayer and meditation was discussed in the first chapter, but since prayer is such an important part of meditation, let us bring it to mind once more.

As preparation is made to enter the Silence, one prays. And one always prays for himself before praying for others. This may seem to be an act of selfishness but it really isn't. Self-prayer is helpful in raising the spiritual vibrations of the body. It also helps to awaken the consciousness and, in turn, gives added power when praying and acting as a channel of blessing for others.

Praying is part of the attuning of the spiritual, mental, and physical bodies.

"Attune yourself almost in the same manner as you tune the violin for harmony. For when the body-mind and the soul-mind is attuned to the infinite, there will be brought harmony to the mind and those centers from which impulse arises will aid in the directing of the individual entity to become more sensitive and the material things about the entity may be the better enjoyed. There will not be brought just what we might call satisfaction." (1861-18)

The body, mind, and soul are all tied together by the miracle of birth, but there are times when the three bodies appear to separate, each seemingly bent on going in a different direction. By the practice of meditation, and focusing on things of a spiritual nature, these three bodies can be brought back into harmony, with each one performing the functions intended for it by its Creator.

"Then use it, not in a boastful manner, but let it make thee humble, even as He, though not other than He, who thought it not robbery to make Himself equal with God. But know that it is not by self, but as the spirit moves in thee, through thy attuning of thy body, thy mind, thy soul, to that consciousness." (1152-9)

Chapter V

THE SEVEN SPIRITUAL CENTERS

To understand even a little of what happens to the physical, mental, and spiritual bodies during the practice of meditation, one must know the part played by the ductless glands of the endocrine system. The glands represent the seven spiritual centers of the body.

A study of the Book of Revelation in the New Testament is highly recommended if one would fully understand the spiritual symbology of the seven centers.

The ductless glands react to a different degree in each individual; that applies to the part that they are involved in in the spiritual awakening, as well as the part they play in the actual physical well being of an individual.

"But there are physical contacts which the anatomist finds not, or those who would look for the imaginations of the mind. Yet it is found that within the body there are channels, there are ducts, there are glands, there are activities that perform no one knows what! in a living,

MOVING, thinking being. In many individuals such have become dormant. Many have become atrophied. Why? Non-usage, non-activity! Because only the desires of the appetite, self-indulgencies and such, have so glossed over or used up the abilities in these directions that they become only wastes as it were in the spiritual life of an individual who has abused or mis-used those abilities that have been given to him for the greater use." (282-41)

The centers, then, which have become dormant through non-usage, will awaken in meditation.

"There has long been sought, by a few, the interpretation of the seven centers; and many have in various stages of awareness, or development, placed the association or connection between physical, mental and spiritual in varied portions of the body. Some have interpreted as the mind, motivated by impulse; and thus called the center from which mind works.

"This is only relatively so, as will be understood by those who analyze those conditions presented through these interpretations; for in fact the body, the mind and the soul are ONE, in the material manifestation. Yet in analyzing them, as given through the Revelation by John, they are active in the various influences that are a part of each living organism conceived in the forces making up that known as man; that power able to conceive—in the mind—of God, and to demonstrate same in relationships to others; that in mind able to conceive of manners for the destruction of its fellow man, little realizing that it is *self* being destroyed by that very activity!" (282-51)

The seven spiritual centers, then, are involved in both

good and evil. In meditation, the power is raised and it is up to each individual what it will be used for. We see that the centers act as influences on each and every part of the living man. Thus it is not difficult to understand the part that the centers have in the cleansing of the mind, and other parts of the physical body, as the energy is raised during meditation.

KUNDALINI

In meditation, it is through the seven spiritual centers that the kundalini flow of energy, or the Sleeping Princess as it is referred to in some philosophies, is awakened. The kundalini is a flow of energy which rises upward from the lowest gland, the gonads, to the pineal and then spills over into the pituitary, the master gland. Also, kundalini is the sanskrit word for Life or Creative Energy.

The kundalini must be brought into movement before one may hope to reach the Christ Consciousness within.

Visualize this tremendous flow of energy as it moves upward through the body from the gonads to the pineal, thence spilling over into the pituitary as "the crook in the staff." As one mentally sees the energy rising, he can see the pituitary as "the cup that overfloweth." Thus it is that we can understand "thy rod and thy staff, they comfort me."

The kundalini doesn't change, "for it is the seat, or the source of life-giving forces in the body. The effect upon the body depends upon the use to which an individual entity puts same. Thus the warning, as was indicated, as to how and for what, such influences are raised within the body itself." (3481-3)

The creative energy can be used for destructive purposes as well as for the betterment of each individual. The purpose for which it is used lies within each person raising it during meditation.

To raise the kundalini in meditation without first spiritualizing the mental body, one cannot hope to derive the proper benefits from the flow.

Also, before attempting to raise the kundalini in meditation, it becomes essential that one make proper preparations of the physical body, especially the breathing exercises as outlined in Chapter II.

For, "Without preparation, desires of EVERY nature may become so accentuated as to destroy—or to overexercise as to bring detrimental forces; unless the desire and purpose is acknowledged and IN the influence of self as to its direction—when loosened by the kundalini activities through the body . . . this opening of the centers or the raising of the life force may be brought about by certain characters of breathing—for, as indicated, the breath is power in itself . . ." (2475-1)

When the kundalini begins to flow through the body, one should "surround self with that consciousness of the Christ Spirit; this by the affirmation of 'Let self be surrounded with the Christ Consciousness,' and the DIRECTION be through those activities in the body-force itself." (2072-11)

It is in the memory cells of the spiritual centers that one will find the resting place of karma, good or bad, the talents, the abilities, the weaknesses, as well as the strengths.

It is in the spiritual centers that the soul-memory impresses and records those aspects of karma which can become active and effect the current activity of individuals.

Thus one can see how it is that as the creative energy moves upward during meditation, memory patterns of long buried activities may be reawakened. It is understandable why it is necessary that one use a spiritual affirmation before entering into meditation. One of the reasons for the affirmation, of course, is that one will wish to spiritualize the mind and reawaken things of a spiritual nature.

"Hence there is in the system that activity of the soul, that is the gift of the Creator to man. It may be easily seen, then, how very closely the glands are associated with reproduction, degeneration; and this throughout— not only the physical forces of the body but the mental body and the soul body.

"The glandular forces, then, are ever akin to the sources from which, through which, the soul dwells within the body." (281-38)

THE GONADS

The gonads are the male and female sex glands. In the male, these particular glands secrete the sperm cell—the life cell of the body. In the female, the gonads secrete the egg cell which must be fertilized at the point of conception for birth.

The gonads also secrete certain hormones which are important not only to vitality, but to the spiritual, mental, and emotional health of an individual. In all probability, it is a minute bit of energy from one of the hormones which is accelerated, thereby starting the upward rise of the kundalini during meditation, since the gonads are the power point of the body.

"Thus, this [the gonads] is the first of the centers from which arises all that is movement, to bring into being both the face and the preface—or the back, or the reverse —in the experience. It carries with it, what? That MIND! For, remember, ever, the pattern is ever the same—Mind the builder." (281-51)

THE CELLS OF LEYDIG

"For, in the body there is that center in which the soul is expressive, creative in its nature—the Leydig center . . .

"As this life force [kundalini flow of energy] is expanded, it moves first from the Leydig center through the adrenals, in what may be termed an upward trend, to the pineal and to the centers in control of emotions—or reflexes through the nerve forces of the body." (2475-1)

In the male, from the cells of Leydig, there is a substance called androgen, which is a sex hormone and is important to the entire life of an individual.

The Leydig center is the starting point for the changes which occur in an individual's body at puberty. There is a possibility that this particular center is involved in the poltergeist phenomena which have been known to occur around certain individuals as they reach the age of puberty. The poltergeist phenomena are of a psychic nature and may be triggered by the opening of this center.

Also, there is a good possibility that the cells of Leydig relate to the male and female balance in individuals.

". . . what takes place in the developing body, or in life growth . . . may be different from that which takes place as one attempts to meditate and to distribute the life force in order to aid another—or to control the influence as in healing, or to attain to an attunement in self for a deeper or better understanding." (281-53)

ADRENALS

The kundalini continues its upward traveling from the Leydig center to the adrenal glands. The adrenals are triangular in shape and sit on top of the kidneys on both sides of the back. They manufacture better than fifty hormone-like substances, including adrenaline. The adrenals are the very essense of life itself.

Frequently referred to as the "fight or flight" glands, the adrenals are responsible for prodigious feats of strength. On the positive side at the adrenal level there is the energy flow having to do with vigor, persistence, and the power to keep driving; also courage. These are actually all different qualities in an individual, but they are all related to the secretions of these particular endocrine glands. Through the negative aspects of the same glands, one will find the arousing of anger, hate, and fear.

Through the adrenal glands come both positive and negative aspects in an individual. Therefore it is under-

standable why it is believed that it is in the cell mind of
the adrenals that the karmic patterns are carried over
from lifetime to lifetime.

In meditation, the adrenal centers are opened and this
could very well be the point where individuals are made
aware of things which could prove to be stumbling blocks
or steppingstones as one moves along the path to the
Christ Consciousness.

It is also interesting to note that many psychic phenomena of different kinds are associated with the adrenal
glands.

The adrenal glands are related to the solar plexus center, the great sun center of the body. Also, these glands
are one of the hard-working vitality centers of the physical body.

THYMUS

From the adrenals the kundalini flow of energy continues its upward wending to the thymus gland, which is
seated above the heart. When an infant is born the thymus weighs about two grams. At the age of puberty the
gland has increased its weight up to twelve, fifteen, or
even twenty grams. By the time an adult has reached the
age of forty to forty-five years of age, the thymus has de-
creased in weight to one or one and one-half grams.

The thymus gland is the seat of personality that uses
self. It is also the seat of love of self and others. The influence of the thymus gland can work for good or bad in an
individual. It represents the evolving principle in man.

The four lower glands in the physical body—gonads,

cells of Leydig, adrenals, and the thymus—represent the physical side of man's nature. This is the side of man that one must strive to overcome in his desire to commune with the Christ Consciousness within.

The three upper spiritual centers are the parathyroid (and the thyroid together in the throat area), the pineal at the top and back of the brain, and the pituitary which hangs at the very front center of the brain.

PARATHYROID/THYROID

As the flow of energy continues upward from the lower centers, it encounters the parathyroid/thyroid glands, the first of the three upper spiritual centers. Metaphysically, or beyond the physical or material, the parathyroid/thyroid centers have charge of the spoken voice. It is from this point that the spoken prayers go forth.

The spiritual centers in the throat area also seem to be closely related to the gift of clairvoyance, or the ability of an individual to know the future before it happens.

The parathyroid/thyroid glands relate to the will and the driving power to make up one's mind, or the ability to choose one way or the other.

"Then within each of the organs themselves (though they each are, in the main, glands) the functioning is stimulated by the activity of each organ's ability to assimilate that needed from the environs, as well as from that upon which it is fed, to grow INTO that direction given BY the mental purpose, the mental desire of the

PERSONALITY—AS it, as an individual, makes itself manifest in a material environ." (281-51)

PINEAL

"Then the next is the pineal, through which the brain forces make manifest . . ." (281-51) It is through the pineal gland that the brain forces or desires are made known.

The pineal should be thought of as the very seat of soul-memory. When this center is opened in meditation, it can re-call to memory all that the soul has been since it was created. It may also bring to memory one's spiritual name. Perhaps this is related to the white stone described in Revelation 2:17: "And I will give him a white stone, and in that stone a name written, which no man knoweth save him that receiveth it."

The pineal is considered the seat of the mind and is of the Christ Consciousness within and without.

PITUITARY

From the pineal, the kundalini energy spills over into the pituitary gland, the master spiritual center, "the cup that overfloweth."

The pituitary is a small, pinkish bit of tissue, hanging like a berry on a little stem from the front underside of the brain. It is extremely sensitive to vibrations of all kinds.

The pituitary is the healing center of the body. Through it is expressed the universal love. The pituitary is that part of the spiritual body which is referred to as the "third eye." It is here that one becomes aware of the Christ Consciousness.

We can choose to express through the glands and open the seven spiritual centers, or we can choose to leave them closed and just be physical. We are always making the choice, consciously or unconsciously.

Upon recognizing the importance of the seven spiritual centers in meditation, an individual might very well ask, "How may I bring into activity my pineal and pituitary glands, as well as the kundalini and other chakras [centers], that I may attain to higher mental and spiritual powers?"

The answer to that question is, "As indicated, first to so FILL the mind with the ideal that it may vibrate throughout the whole of the MENTAL being!

"Then, close the desires of the fleshly self to conditions about same. MEDITATE upon 'THY WILL WITH ME.' Feel same. Fill ALL the centers of the body, the lowest to the highest, with that ideal; opening the centers by surrounding self first with that consciousness, 'NOT MY WILL BUT THINE, O LORD, BE DONE IN AND THROUGH ME.'

"And then, have that desire, that purpose, not of attaining without HIS direction, but WITH His direction, who is the Maker, the Giver of life and light; as it is indeed in Him that we live and move and have our being." (1861-4)

In meditation, then, the kundalini flow of creative energy is raised from the lowest physical center, the gonads, to the master spiritual center, the pituitary. Upon reaching the master center, the energy rises above the common matter of the physical and mental bodies, touches upon the spirit body, overflows and comes back to cleanse and heal.

In the rising of the energy from center to center, it may be felt as a "quickening" or a great rapidity within the body. There will be times when one is not aware that the energy is rising until it culminates in the pituitary and the white light suddenly breaks forth in all of its glory. At times the very essence of the body seems to expand and feel as if the skin containing it might break and split into a million pieces.

Do not become discouraged if, upon meditating day after day, nothing happens. It does take patience. Remember, ". . . As has so oft been indicated, . . . it is as we use that in hand that the greater opportunities are given." (1472-9)

It is in perseverance and not giving up, in using the adrenal glands on the positive side, that the consciousness begins to develop on a higher plane and meditation becomes that which is sought.

One should understand that meditation is not just a matter of sitting still for a given period of time with an attitude of expectancy. It must be realized, "In the material plane the raising of the mental consciousness to the various spheres of attunement is accomplished only in concentration and in attuning self to those forces as are without. The body-consciousness is made up, as has been given, of more than *one* consciousness—as is flesh, as is body—for there is the physical body, there is the mental body, there is the spiritual body. There is the spiritual consciousness, there is the mental consciousness, there is the body consciousness. These have their various minds or *planes*, as may be seen. As one develops, or as one opens self in those various spheres of understanding, one attains or gains an access, a vision, an insight, a hearing, a feeling, into those various planes. By the use of that in hand does one attain the next plane. The preparation for tomorrow is builded on today." (5472-1)

In the opening of the seven spiritual centers, each individual will have different experiences. The interpretation which one individual might give to an experience will not necessarily apply to another's experience. In this chapter, we have tried to bring to the reader's understanding the primary symbolic points as related to each center. As in all things, with all individuals God's gift of free will will take precedence over everything else. It is what one does with the knowledge gained through study and meditation that will direct each one.

". . . but each individual's *experience* in the application of that gained by each in his or her experience will be different. To give an interpretation that the opening or activity through a center raises or means or applies this or that, then would become rote. But know the way, then each may apply same as his or her environment, ability, experience, gives the opportunity. For know, in all and through all, the activity of self is only as a channel—and God giveth the understanding, the increase, to such; and in the manner as is best fitted for the individual. It is not then as a formula, that there are to be certain activities and certain results. These are true in the sense that they each represent or present the opportunity for the opening to the understanding of the individual, but the application is as to the individual. For, as has been given, man is free-willed. And only when this is entirely given, and actively given, to the will of the Father may be even as the life of the Christ." (281-29)

SYMBOLOGY OF THE CENTERS

Symbolic evidence of the seven spiritual centers may be found in many places. For instance, in studying what is said by John in the Book of Revelation, it becomes simply a matter of applying the centers to the seven churches which are spoken of: Gonads—Ephesus; Cells of Leydig—Smyrna; Adrenals—Pergamus; Thymus—Thyatira; Parathyroid/Thyroid—Sardis; Pineal—Philadelphia; and finally the master gland, Pituitary—Laodicea.

Also, in the seven churches there are seven candlesticks on the altars. And in the Episcopal church the censer is swung out toward the congregation seven times. Could this be to bring to the remembrance the seven spiritual centers of the physical body?

The first four lower centers of the body may be related to the four horses in Revelation: Gonads—White Horse; Cells of Leydig—Black Horse; Adrenals—Red Horse; Thymus—Pale Horse.

The seven spiritual centers may also be symbolized in The Lord's Prayer. Too, each center is believed to have its own governing color:

PITUITARY	Father /Heaven	Violet
PINEAL	Son /Name	Indigo
PARATHYROID/THYROID	Holy Spirit /Will	Blue
THYMUS	Evil /Love	Green
ADRENALS	Debts /Balance	Yellow
CELLS OF LEYDIG	Temptation /Lift	Orange
GONADS	Bread /Strength	Red

Also, there is Mohammed's vision of the golden rope which hung down from heaven with the seven knots in it. Think of the seven knots as the seven spiritual centers. Each time a center is opened, one climbs toward heaven, or attunement with the Master.

In meditation one learns to climb the golden rope, knot by knot, cleansing and healing the centers of the body as one moves upward. In the centers are stored all of the blocks, all of the fears, as well as all of the power, talents and abilities waiting to be tapped.

In meditation one seeks the ability to cope with the mental and physical strain that each imposes upon himself. With the awakening to the Christ Consciousness within, one learns to live with himself and others.

Jesus, the Christ, said that the Kingdom of God is within. Therefore, in turning within during meditation one finds the key to open the door from whence comes all well-being for the physical, the mental, the soul.

Chapter VI

EXPERIENCES ALONG THE WAY

As one begins to attain the ability to still the body and mind during meditation, they will begin to have a variety of experiences. Vibrations of the body may be felt as a swaying or circular motion. Sounds may begin to come from out of nowhere. Visions, or scenes, may be seen during meditation. Some individuals will become aware of odors and fragrances for which there docs not seem to be an answer. Most of these experiences are from the unconscious and should be thought of as signposts along the way.

The majority of the experiences will happen because the five senses are more acute as a result of meditation. Needless to say, this will not apply to all of the experiences; some are very definitely of a spiritual nature.

As one becomes aware of the experiences during meditation, gently but firmly bring the attention back to the spiritual affirmation. Try not to let the experiences become distracting or lead one from the purpose of meditation.

After coming out of meditation, try to interpret the happening, try to relate it to something that might be happening in your own personal life. The experience may be symbolic and tend to defy understanding for the moment. But the longer one works with meditation and the many things which will happen, the clearer the symbology will become.

Bear in mind that the same experience may not always mean the same thing to everyone. For example, a red rose may mean love and happiness to one individual; to another it might signify death and unhappiness. Also, the red of the rose could be related to anger and the adrenal glands. Perhaps the anger is not even a current one but one that has been hidden in the unconscious and has come to the front after a long time of being buried. If this is so, the buried feeling should be taken out, looked at and learned from. This is one of the many ways an individual can grow in understanding himself and others.

There may be times when the visions experienced are fragments of a past life. This could happen as the result of opening the spiritual centers; the triggering of certain soul-memories which are seated in various centers.

BODY MOVEMENTS

One of the more frequent happenings which is experienced by individuals during meditation is an involuntary movement or vibration of the physical body.

"If these movements are from that which may be controlled within thy own imagination, well to be controlled. If these are from zeal, effort and power as from on High, let Him have His way with thee. Be sure in self these do not arise from self-emotion, but emotion from without. These, as indicated by this given, then at times may be controlled by self and are self's own emotions; at others they are as ringing ever, 'Neither do I condemn thee'; neither hast thou been one through whom condemnations have come to any since His blessings have been on thee! Keep thine self in body pure from contaminations with those of unbelievers. Keep thine mind as a channel for His expressions of love, and you will find that He will walk, will talk with thee—even as in the garden." (295-9)

In the above reading, an individual was told that the body movement could be of the imagination; if so, then curb it. It could also be caused as the result of the attunement with the Master. Should the latter be the case, then the individual should let himself become as a channel of blessings for others.

There are spiritual vibrations of the body which can occur during meditation and these are not to be confused with the ones caused by an overactive desire to deliberately cause them.

One bodily movement is a swaying of the upper torso. Another is a backward and forward movement whereby the body will feel as if it is rocking. There is a certain primitive soothing of the body when this occurs. The rocking may originate as the result of the imagination or it could come from other sources, which have been tapped during meditation.

A few years back, when I was living in an apartment in New York, I was sitting in the lotus position on the floor, meditating. My physical body seemed to pick up a backward and forward rocking movement. In my mind's eye I could see the body actually moving across the floor, out the terrace door and dropping eleven floors to the street below. My eyes flew open and, of course, I was still in the exact spot I was when I had gone into meditation.

In the particular experience just described, I had so completely forgotten my purpose and concentrated on the movements of the body that I had caused them to increase. In my opinion, these movements at that time were not of a spiritual nature but were caused by mental and physical fatigue. Because of the soothing of the body by the rocking, I had unconsciously increased it.

When one is meditating with a healing purpose in mind for another, a different type of vibration may occur. Cayce was asked about this: "How can one direct the vibration culminating in the head to the one they would aid?"

The reply was, "By *thought*. (Now we are speaking of a purely mechanical, metaphysical-spiritual activity that would take place.) One has directed their thought to an individual who is to receive the blessing of that power or force raised. They raise within themselves that which may be sent out as a power, and it passes to those that would be in attune or accord. Were they present a much greater force may be felt, to be sure; less is the strain upon the physical body." (281-14)

In the projection of healing thought to another, a very real power has been raised within the individual and it is this power which is being sent out to aid. The individual is then acting as a channel of healing.

Quite a few questions have been asked about vibrations which occur during meditation, including the following: "During meditation I have experienced a strong vibration. The whole body rocking. Please explain. And have I been able to direct this current to those we are trying to aid?"

The answer was: "As the vibrations are raised within self through this very visualization, this experiencing of there being those activities, the body—and everyone—is able to send, or direct, or create an environ—to such an one to whom the thought is directed—that is helpful, hopeful, beneficial in every way." (281-15)

There is another type of vibration which happens when one is aware of the sheer beauty of drawing nearer to the Master. Such an experience is described in the following reading: ". . . my whole body seemed to be vibrating to the thought that I had opened my heart to the unseen forces that surround the throne of grace, and beauty, and might, and throwing about self that protection that is found in thoughts of Him. Please explain."

The experience was explained thus: "Just as has been given, the nearer one—a body, this body—draws to that complete consciousness that is in Him, the greater may be the power—that is manifested through His presence in the world through that as is brought about in self's own experience. The more forceful, the more helpful, does the body become at such, and through such, experiences. Let these remain as sacred experiences, gathering more and

more of same—but as such is given out, so does it come."
(281-5)

In spiritualizing the body, the mind, and the soul, as
in preparation for meditation with the ideals, affirmations, and in raising the kundalini in the opening of the
spiritual centers, one does draw nearer to the Christ
Consciousness within and without. By the sharing of this
blessing by helping others, one may become doubly
blessed and the beauty of knowing Him will be even
greater.

SLEEP

Some individuals report that they have fallen asleep
during meditation. There is also the feeling of wondering
if one has fallen asleep. These individuals tend to have
a feeling of disappointment that this has happened. They
also wonder why it happened.

This is "Perfect relaxation. There is gradually the taking hold by the inner forces, or inner powers of the body.
Train, or set self to retain more and more that which is
experienced through such sleep, or such loss of consciousness; for activation is taking place. Remember, the
heart doesn't stop beating because you are asleep. The
brain doesn't stop acting because you are asleep. Remember all forces; for sleep is as a *sense* of the whole
system, and is the great recuperating force. When considered in the same manner, the senses of touch, of seeing, of hearing, of feeling, of all the forces within self,
are just as helpful in bringing recuperation, if the di-

versions are as such a way and manner acted upon to rebuild rather than to destroy all force or strength in the physical body—see? so, in the activating of that sense of sleep, the auditory forces—or those that come through feeling and hearing (which are on guard before the throne then), then harken to that which is received, even as listening to the program of the best salesman you have sent out! for it *is* the best! for it's before the Throne!" (257-92)

Meditation tends to make one more sensitive to remembering and picking up things which happen during sleep. It is in sleep that an individual may very well have the ability to break the time-space barriers which exist.

VARIETY OF EXPERIENCES

It is well that an individual not force any of the experiences which he may have during meditation. If they are going to happen, they should be allowed to do so of their own accord. Analyze, learn, and grow from the experiences. And help others to do the same.

The following are examples of a variety of experiences which different individuals have experienced during meditation. Most of the answers given by Edgar Cayce are self-explanatory.

An explanation was requested by an individual who had experienced a pumping sensation in the lower part of the spine during meditation.

"As has been given, as to how those forces in the system are the channels through which the activating sensations arise through those forces of the body for transmission to those portions of the physical body from which sensations are sent out for the activating forces *in* the physical bodies, then these are but the samples, or the attempts of those forces to rise to their activities in the consciousness of the body. Do not force same, but so conduct the mind's trend, the body's activities, as to leave self a channel for such expressions." (281-12)

It would seem, with this particular experience, that the person is being told to cleanse the mind and body in a spiritual manner, and let the force rise of its own accord. The self will then be a channel for the necessary expressions, whether this be healing for another, or whatever is the purpose of the rising of the force which is causing the sensations in the spine.

Since the pituitary is thought of as being in the vicinity of the center forehead, it is not unusual for one to experience certain sensations in that area as the kundalini rises and spills over into that master center.

Many individuals have experienced sensations involving the eyes and the area around them. An example is given in the following request and answer: "Please explain the physical experiences in connection with the eyes, that have been the result of meditation."

"We have the body, the mind, the soul. The soul is eternal. As to how eternal the mind is depends upon its creative influence, or as to how eternal it remains.

"Then, when there is the subjugation of the physical through the mental and spiritual, the flow of the eternal is through—and to—those portions of the body to which such suggestions are directed.

"For, know that all HEALING—whether it is through the application of mechanical, mental or spiritual forces—comes from the one source. For it is indeed as He has given, 'In Him ye live and move and have thy being.'" (1861-5)

This individual, in raising the creative flow of energy while meditating, actually felt the sensation in the area of the eyes. As the kundalini is raised, there may also be physical sounds. This may be attributed to blocks falling away and the centers opening, or physical hindrances being removed.

For instance, a meditator experienced what seemed like the opening and shutting of a valve in the forehead. The sound was actually heard by another person in the room.

This sound had to do with the opening of the spiritual centers—along the cord of life—in the physical body. ". . . and—as there were physical obstructions—produced a physical sound when opened by the raising of the vibrations through the body.

"This and such experiences then become *assurances;* not boastful, not overlording, but producing in the positive consciousness the physical activity of which you have a mental knowledge." (281-35)

As the spiritual centers are opened and the blocks, physical, mental, spiritual, which have been built over a long period of time begin to no longer constitute a hazard, one will know that he is drawing closer to the Christ Consciousness within.

So many different levels of consciousness are tapped during meditation that it may become difficult for an individual to know which level he is attuned to. One person reported that during meditation there was a cool feeling as if something had been placed upon the head and forehead, extending down the nose.

The explanation for this experience was, "As would be termed—literal—as the breath of an angel, or the breath of a master. As the body attunes self, as has been given, it may be a channel where there may be even *instant* healing with the laying on of hands. The more often this occurs, the more *power* is there felt in the body, the more forcefulness in the act or word." (281-5)

Another experience might be likened to the "brush of an angel's wing." While in meditation, it is not unusual to become aware of something lightly brushing the hair or face. Perhaps we are sometimes in the presence of angels; God did give them charge over His children.

BEING AWARE OF THE MASTER

Over the many years there are untold numbers of times whereby people have reported seeing the Master or being aware of His presence. Some have seen Him during meditation; others have been aware of Him as they go about their business. He has manifested in many ways to many different people. He comes in times of joy as well as during periods of great tribulations.

There are times, too, when an individual may be made aware of that which represents Him, as in the following where one reported that she had seen the Master walking in a garden, and asked for an interpretation of the experience.

"In the meditation were the experiences of the awareness of that which separated itself. . . . The separation of light from the source of light, that manifested itself in the material, the mental and spiritual world. The walking in the garden represents the figure of the oneness of purpose, the closeness to that source of light to those that seek to know the way as He would have each one go.

"Hence more and more there may come to those that seek the experiences that to them represent or give the better interpretation and understanding of that they seek in the study of the way He, the Master, would have them go. . . ." (262-56)

Nearly everyone, at one time or another, has thought that he has heard his name called. He answers, but there isn't anyone there, or so he thinks.

"As there have oft been the experiences of individuals being called by the mentors, or those guards of the various forces as manifest in the material world, so may the call come to one who has set self in body-mind to serve, that is called to service. So, in the experience, the body-consciousness was called by Him as would guide, direct, who is the way, the light, that leads to the proper conception of relationships in the various elements of life itself. A call from Him, who called, 'Martha, know ye not she hath chosen the better part?'" (281-12)

Being called, seeing, or just becoming aware of His presence happens time and time again. There are times when one is not aware of why he was summoned.

There are times, too, when the physical, the mental, the spiritual bodies, are in dire need of comfort and it comes from Him.

The following excerpt is from a letter written by Edgar Cayce to a friend.

"Often I have felt, seen and heard the Master at hand. Just a few days ago I had an experience which I have not even told the folks here. As you say, they are too scary to tell, and we wonder at ourselves when we attempt to put them into words, whether we are to believe our own ears, or if others feel we are exaggerating or drawing on our imagination; but to us indeed they are often that which we feel if we hadn't experienced we could not have gone on.

"The past week I had been quite 'out of the running,' but Wednesday afternoon when going into my little office or den for the 4:45 meditation, as I knelt by my couch I had the following experience: First a light gradually filled the room with a golden glow that seemed to be very exhilarating, putting me in a buoyant state. I felt as if I were being given a healing. Then, as I was about to give the credit to members of our own group who meet at this hour for meditation (as I felt each and everyone of them were praying for and with me), HE came. He stood before me for a few minutes in all the glory that He must have appeared in to the three on the Mount. Like yourself I heard the voice of my Jesus say, 'Come unto me and rest.'"

How does one tell another that he has known the presence of the Master? Needless to say, the first inclination is to share the jubilant experience with others. With joy, one would like to shout it from the housetops. Unfortunately, it does not work that way. Eventually, one realizes that the experience was personal and that it is best to let it remain as a sacred experience. But it can be shared in another way. From an experience of this nature, one will grow closer to the Master, growing in understanding of others and will want to give of himself to help others grow and reach the same experience on their own.

INTERPRETING OF EXPERIENCES

There are various ways of interpreting experiences which may happen during meditation and the things which one will encounter as he draws nearer to the Christ Spirit. Most experiences will represent different things to different individuals. It is to the personal advantage of each individual if he will learn to work with the symbology involved.

There are many different sources from which one might work. One of the best is the Edgar Cayce "Search for God" groups, which are now international. The Cayce readings at the Association for Research and Enlightenment, Virginia Beach, Virginia, are an excellent source of interpretation. The Bible can also serve as a guideline in working with meditation experiences.

As an example of how one might go about interpreting an experience: Two individuals, while in group meditation, had the same identical experience at the same time. They both became aware of breaking through to the white light, and both people said it was slashed through with a flaming sword.

In Genesis 4:24, it is written, "So he drove out the man; and he placed at the east of the garden of Eden Cherubims, and a flaming sword which turned every way, to keep the tree of life."

The Metaphysical Bible Dictionary explains the flaming sword in depth, saying, "I AM is the gate through which the thinker comes forth from the invisible to the visible, and it is through this gate that he must go to get into the presence of Spirit. 'I am the way, and the truth, and the life.' Hence we take words and go to God. We came out from His presence through the I AM [free will] gate, and we must return the same way. On the inner side of the gate is the Garden of Eden, but 'the Cherubim and the flame of a sword' are there 'to keep the way of the tree of life.' The flame of a sword 'is the inner motive that rules our thoughts and acts. It turns every way to guard the tree of life, for the tree of life is the precious substance of the Father.'"

In this experience of the two people seeing the flaming sword cutting through the white light, it can be interpreted that the I AM gate represents free will. The sword is capable of turning every way, not only to guard the tree of life but it also rules "our thoughts and acts," which are the manifested results of the free will.

It would seem that these two individuals were being shown very clearly that God waited for them, but to reach Him they must *choose freely* to return.

In meditation, one lets go of free will through choice. Sometimes we find it hard to let go of the ego, to say,

"I'm yours. Guide me, direct me, O Lord. Let Thy will be done, not mine." It is in the letting go that individuals find their way back to Him.

With the expansion of spiritual awareness, the physical senses become keener and one is more likely to become aware of certain things which might have gone unnoticed prior to the new growth. With this newly developed awareness, the meditator will find that he is beginning to have varied and, to him, new experiences. Do not dwell upon them but interpret them to the best of one's ability and use them for the purpose for which they were meant. Think of the experiences as serendipities—not ends in themselves.

"These are, then, as experiences. Learn ye to use them, for they will give expressions in many ways and manners. Seek experiences not as experiences alone but as purpose-fulness. For what be the profit to thyself, to thy neighbor, if experiences alone of such nature rack thy body . . . owing to its high vibration . . . without being able to make thee a kinder mother, a more loving wife, a better neighbor, a better individual in every manner? *These* be the fruits, that make thee kinder, gentler, stronger in body, in mind, in purpose to *be* a channel through which the love of *God*, through Jesus Christ, may be manifested in the world. Not as a vision, an experience alone."
(281-27)

Chapter VII

GROUP MEDITATION

To understand fully the growth of spirituality, it becomes necessary to comprehend the universe as a whole and know that each individual is a vital part of it. As each person grows in his own way, he helps someone else to grow. For individuals to grow spiritually, each must be willing to lean upon another, and, in turn, be willing to offer the same help.

In realizing that everything that moves, lives, and has its being in the universe, is part of the one Creator, one is then able to clearly grasp his own connection to his fellow man, and vice versa. In coming together, then, one sees the strength that is gained, and put forth, through group meditation and prayer.

As each individual grows in knowledge and understanding, those who are working with him also grow. If there is a common purpose or goal which the group is praying and meditating about, greater strength will be given to it.

When consistently praying and meditating with the same group of individuals, it is not at all unusual to discover genuine love and concern developing, one for the other. It is almost as if an invisible chain links the members of the group together, one to the other. Frequently, extrasensory perception (ESP) begins to develop within the group with each member becoming attuned to the others.

Concern begins to build within the group not only for each other, but for mankind as a whole. By showing love and concern for others, each individual not only contributes to his own growth but to the growth of the other persons. And, not surprisingly, meditation begins to improve. For, "By being as given, more and more patient, more and more longsuffering, more and more tolerant, more and more *lovely* to every one ye meet in *every* way ye act, in every word ye *speak*, in every thought ye think," (272-9) thus does man draw closer to the Christ Consciousness and the universe as a whole. It is then that consciousness of all that is awakens.

Each individual brings to the group his own experiences, problems, and opportunities. As he has learned from each experience, so may the others share his knowledge and growth. As, ". . . there is much that may be accomplished through the exercising of that knowledge which is in the experience of many. In the application will come understanding and greater abilities for the exercising of that which is gained through the varied and various experiences of all." (281-6)

Among a group working together on one purpose in prayer and meditation there is a strong non-verbal communication in terms of healing. This would apply not only to physical healing, but to other types of healing as well such as economic, world peace, marital difficulties, or whatever may present itself.

Understanding that thoughts are things and that they carry power as strongly as any solidly built item will help the group members to recognize what is happening when it, the group, is of one accord in its prayers and meditations.

Also, there may be times when an individual may be inclined to strike out on his own, or pull away from the group he is working with. Should this happen, the group can help to pull him back on the right course and prevent him from becoming lost in a maze of confusion.

As Cayce said, "Let that rather be thy watchword, 'I am my brother's keeper.' Who is thy brother? Whoever, wherever he is, that bears the imprint of the Maker in the earth, be he black, white, gray or grizzled, be he young, be he Hottentot, or on the throne or in the president's chair. All that are in the earth today are thy brothers." (2780-3)

GROUP TIME

It is not very often that the same group of individuals can meet every day for the period of meditation. However, they should arrange to meet at least once a week. If meditation is a group effort, a time convenient to all should be set aside and each individual pray and meditate wherever he may be.

In making preparation for a study group, there must be wholehearted co-operation, ". . . whether in meditation, in thought, in act, or what; for, as is given, the *union* of strength may accomplish much, even in the activities that may be accomplished in *any* phase of life, whether the spiritual life, or material life, the imaginative life or the spiritual; for, as the forces run, in the active principles they must be that as is motivative, that as is the carrier, that as is accomplished.

"So, keep in the way and manner as has been *outlined*, and be faithful—each—to that portion. Think none that their dependence must be upon another. Put rather the dependence in the *Father* . . .

"In the meditations—we would set as a specific time for all to meditate; for he that may not cooperate one with another has little part in that that may be accomplished; for whether these be much or little, their activity —in accord—keeps harmony; harmony makes for peace; peace for understanding; understanding for enlightenment. In *this*, then, let all be active." (262-4)

GROUP EXPERIENCES

Every member of a group should not be disappointed if he does not have experiences of the same nature as the other members. It is necessary to realize that the same degree of growth and understanding will not be achieved by all members simultaneously.

"If one begins and all join, wonderful; but do not find fault that all are not in attune at once. Were all chosen to go into the chamber of death? Were all chosen to go to the mount of transfiguration? Were All chosen to act when the five thousand were fed? There you find, in the various experiences, numbers or a different one among the twelve taking the leading role—as you do at the Last Supper, as you do at the Cross, as you do in the Garden, as you do on Resurrection Morn." (281-35)

Thus it is stated that each individual is called for a different role at a different time. Therefore, there will be varying degrees of growth and enlightenment among the different members of the group. That is not to say that it indicates a greater or lesser degree of spiritual advancement in any way. To each in his own time is given the right amount of knowledge for the job in hand.

There will be a tendency to discuss various experiences which have happened among the group members. This is all right provided it is not done in a boastfull or bragging manner, nor in a manner which might be inclined to discourage someone who might not have had an experience which he feels is worth discussing.

Group discussions can be very helpful in the interpretation of different experiences. Do not let this reach the stage where it becomes the focal point of the meeting and all lose sight of the original purpose of study, prayer, and meditation.

In group experiences, bear in mind that "Oft we find individual activity becomes so personal in even the meditations that there is sought that this or that, which may have been reported to have happened to another, *must* be the manner of happening to self. And in this manner there is cut away, there is built the barrier which prevents the real inner self from *experiencing*. Let self *loose,* as it were; for thy prayer ascends to the throne of grace, ever; only as self, thought, metes out to thy fellow man. Do not *try,* or crave, or desire a sign; for *thou* art in *thyself* a sign of that thou dost worship within thine inner self! For thou, as every soul, dost stand before the door of the temple where thy God hath promised to meet thee. Then, do not be impatient. For what thou asketh in secret shall be proclaimed from the housetop." (705-2)

Each individual must go within and meet his Creator in his own way and in his own time. There are those who will tap timidly at the door while others may pound boldly. It matters not what happens along the way for each soul is a sign that the Creator waits for the door to be opened.

Do not let the time set aside for group meditation become nothing more than a habit, or a feeling of having to do it. Nor should it be used as an excuse to escape daily tasks. Meditation should never be practiced because one has fallen into the habit and has a sense of guilt if he misses a period. Meditation, whether alone or as part of a group, should be practiced because one wants to do it with all of his heart.

One way to eliminate the feeling that meditation is becoming little more than habit is "By visualizing in such manners those meditations that are given out for others, for self; for in aiding others does one aid one's self most. And unless this is so visualized from within self, it be-

comes rote. But when made, set, or so experienced by
the inner self as being an active, living principle within
self, it ceases to become rote." (281-15)

TRUTH

Everyone is not able to join a group for study, prayer,
and meditation for a number of reasons, including health,
locale, transportation, or whatever the reason may be. But
there should not be any reason why one cannot go within
and join the search for Truth. It exists within each individual as the Christ Consciousness and is there for all
who seek.

Each entity must eventually release the emotional
links which chain him to material elements only. When
one has learned the meaning and the way of letting "self"
go, however briefly, it is then that Truth awakens and the
still small voice of the Master may be heard within.

To know Truth is to know the Master. "Truth is as experience. Hence IS an earning, through the manners in
which a finite mind becomes conscious of what Truth is.
Hence Truth is a growth, and hence an EARNING, a
yearning, a growing, and is EARNED by he or she that
applies that known in the manner that IS in keeping with
His Will, rather than that there may be the satisfying of
self's own desires. Not that man should deny that this
or that force exists, to make self believe, but rather that
the Truth is as that which may be earned through the
EXPERIENCING of the knowledge and understanding
concerning the laws of Truth; for *HE* is *Truth!*" (262-19)

Truth may slip into the consciousness quietly, moving so softly and easily that one is scarcely aware of it. Or it may come with what will seem like a great clash of cymbals, obliterating all else. However it may manifest itself is of little consequence. What is of importance is the recognition of IT.

It is well to know that once Truth has been glimpsed and recognized, never again can It be successfully buried in the subconscious. One may turn from Truth, renounce It, attempt to hide from It, but it will all be to no avail. Never again can the individual who has known Truth hide from the knowledge which comes with the spiritual enlightenment of having found it.

As He is with each individual, so He is with groups who are gathered together in His name, either in the physical or mental, who pray and meditate for each other and for others.

That with which each person approaches such an hour is how much each may contribute to the gathering and receive from it.

"First, let each enter into its own inner self and ask for direction, and—*believing* His presence will be with thee. For, He has promised, 'Where two or three are gathered together in *my* name, *there* I will be in the midst of them.'

"Let each, then, so consecrate, so dedicate that hour, that period, to such a service for its fellow man, seeking, knowing, that His presence will be with thee. Then, when He has directed thine group, who—WHO—would question same?" (281-20)

Chapter VIII

WARNINGS

Everyone should recognize that he is living in a world of duality and that for every positive force there is a negative one. In the inward seeking for the voice of the Master, it is not an uncommon occurrence to encounter forces along the way which would be inclined to deter the search.

With the opening of the seven spiritual centers during meditation, different things may happen to the physical, mental, and soul bodies. It is necessary to take the precaution of keeping these vital centers closed to negative elements, and to properly prepare oneself, physically, mentally, spiritually before going into meditation. One must always bear in mind that it is the Christ Spirit which is sought; one must never be willing to settle for anything less.

One should never plunge blindly into meditation but "Know where you are going before you start out, in

analyzing spiritual and mental and material things."
(3428-1) This is one of the reasons for setting the ideals
in writing and ever so often referring back to them. As
one begins to grow spiritually through the practice of
meditation, the ideals will change. And, as has been
said, be alert for the changes and rewrite them accordingly.

There is also protection in the spiritual affirmations
which are used in meditation. And additional protection
is gained when one mentally surrounds self with the protective light of the Father.

Whether one admits the existence of dark forces or not
is of relatively little importance. The fact is they do exist and can have tremendous power.

An individual, through the Law of Attraction, will at-
tract only those things to which he himself is attracted.
"It, that energy, seeks—by the natural law—that to which
it has an affinity. Affinity is the ideal, then." (826-11)

Therefore, it is logical to realize that one should set
his spiritual ideals and goals to the very highest stand-
ards. "If that mental self, that portion of the Spirit is in
accord with the Divine Will—by its application of its
knowledge as to its relationships to the fellow man in the
manners and purposes as indicated—there comes that
consciousness, that awareness that His Spirit indeed beareth witness with thy spirit." (826-11)

Those who are seeking but know not what is being
sought are sometimes prime targets for discarnate enti-
ties with a negative twist. The dark forces also have a
way of being drawn, or attracted, to individuals who are
emotionally disturbed. For, ". . . there are disturbances

with this body. Much of these, however, are tied up with the emotional natures of this body. And here we find some of those conditions of which many bodies should be warned—the opening of centers in the body—spiritual without correctly directing same, which may oft lead to wrecking of the body—physical and sometimes mental." (3428-1)

Thus it may be through the opening of the spiritual centers without correctly directing them that one may become involved in things which can lead to disturbances of different natures.

POSSESSION

The possession of the body and mind by a discarnate entity is an awesome thing. It may eventually destroy the physical and mental bodies of the individual who is possessed. A medical diagnosis of one who is possessed would classify that individual as a schizophrenic, complete with split personality and dissociation.

It is also well to know that what is sometimes thought of as possession could also be something which may have been buried in an individual's own unconscious.

A young man I will call Bill, experienced what was believed to be possession by a discarnate entity. I was a witness to this particular case over a period of months and it was frightening to watch the disintegration of this young man.

Bill is an exceptionally intelligent individual with an I.Q. bordering on that of genius. He is musically talented

and interested in a wide variety of things. Prior to turning to spiritual meditation, he had bought a very old out-
of-print book on ancient black witchcraft. Bill had studied the book rather thoroughly and had found that some
of the experiments actually worked. When he realized
that he could really do some of the things described in
the old book, he recognized the horror of it and burned
the book.

When Bill turned to spiritual meditation instead of
practicing witchcraft, he learned it very quickly. Basi-
cally, he is of a spiritual nature and had never questioned
the existence of a Supreme Being. But with his natural
curiosity, he began to experiment with meditation. It
was here that he really ran into trouble. He skipped all
of the spiritual aspects of meditation and managed to
open the centers in another manner. Before he fully
realized what could happen to him, he had attracted an
evil influence. There is also the possibility that something
remained in his unconscious from his previous study of
witchcraft.

In any event, in the beginning there were fleeting encounters with what seemed like various discarnate en-
tities, but apparently none were strong enough to control Bill's personality. However, there was eventually one
which took total possession of his mind and body. The
possession was so complete that Bill was never quite sure
whether it was the entity or himself that was speaking
or acting. Bill reached an apathetic state where he was
devoid of feelings and emotions of any kind.

Bill could not sleep without being awakened at odd
hours of the night. He would wander around the house

at all hours of the night and day, with a strange expression on his face. Those around this young man feared for his safety, as well as their own, never quite sure of what he would do next.

Everything Bill tried to eat, he regurgitated almost immediately. During the first two weeks of the possession, he lost twelve pounds. He was on the very brink of total insanity and was fast becoming a physical wreck.

However, Bill is one of the more fortunate ones. He was eventually made to realize what had happened to him and why. Today, more than a year later, this young man is just starting to return to his normal personality and way of life.

It has been a long, hard struggle for Bill, and all so unnecessary. Had he not experimented with evil and dark forces, he would not have attracted one to himself. Had he used his spiritual knowledge as he should have, he would not have encountered anything but good from the Divine within.

One of the Cayce readings gives an excellent description of possession and the gaining of knowledge without making practical application of it.

"We find that there has been the opening of the Lyden (Cells of Leydig) gland, so that the kundalini forces move along the spine to the various centers that open with this attitude, or with these activities of the mental and spiritual forces of the body—much in the same manner as might be illustrated in the foetus that forms from conception. These naturally take form. Hence these take form, for they have not in their inception been put to a definite use.

"The psychological reaction is much like that as may be illustrated in one gaining much knowledge without making practical application of it. It then forms its own concepts.

"Now we combine these two and we have that indicated here as a possession of the body; gnawing, as it were, on all of the seven centers of the body, causing the inability for rest or even a concerted activity—unless the body finds itself needed for someone else. Then the body finds, as this occurs, the disturbance is retarded or fades —in the abilities of the body to exercise itself in help for others." (3421-1)

It is not meditation which causes the difficulties, but rather the manner in which the knowledge gained is used. Once individuals have learned to enter the Silence, the benefits are immeasurable. A peace of mind and glowing well-being descends upon one that cannot be found in any other way of life.

Therefore, to prevent physical and mental harm, ". . . attune self in body and in mind with that influence by which the entity seeks to be directed; not haphazardly, not by chance, but—as of old—choose thou this day WHOM ye will serve; the living God within thee, by thee, through thee? or those influences of knowledge without wisdom, that would enslave or empower thee with the material things which only gratify for the moment?

"Rather choose thou as he of old—let others do as they may, but as for thee, serve thou the living God." (2475-1)

There should be no fear of possession if the wrong obstacles are removed from the path of the seeker. Rather know that dark influences are attracted, "Only so far as resentments are held by self towards others, as has been indicated. And if such cause hate, malice, jealousy, fear and doubt, are removed from [thy] own mind towards others, no influence without or within may be of a detrimental force to self; so long as self will surround self with the thought and the ability of the Christ Consiousness, and then practice same in its dealings with its fellow man.

"No need to proclaim it alone—but live same, daily." (2081-2)

AUTOMATIC WRITING

As one begins to go deeper and deeper into the practice of meditation, formerly closed-off abilities have a very good chance of emerging. In making use of these newly discovered talents, it is advised to do so with caution. "Thus ye may use that ability or spiritual attainment which is the birthright of every soul; ye may use it as a helpful influence in thy experience in the earth.

"But make haste SLOWLY! Prepare the body. Prepare the mind, before ye attempt to loosen it in such measures [or] manners that it may be taken hold upon by those influences which constantly seek expressions of self rather than of a living, constructive influence of a CRUCIFIED Savior." (2475-1)

It is not always easy to know where the talent is coming from. One individual wanted to know, "Are the inspirational writings I receive to be relied upon as coming from a worthy and high source or should I not cultivate this form of guidance and information?"

He was warned, as should everyone be, "We would NOT from here counsel anyone to be guided by influences from without. For the KINGDOM is from within!

"If these come as inspirational writings from within, and not as guidance from others. That is different." (1602-1)

Automatic writing is a means of writing generally without the concurrence and will on the part of the one being used by a discarnate entity. The individual being used may be swayed in many directions, as well as being the means of misleading others.

The following is an example of the kind of thoughts which began to fill one man's mind as he experimented with automatic writing:

> The wind has been blowing in my mind for many years now, but only in this life since death.
> It was a pale crystalline morning. A morning where the amber sun kisses the soft lit blue of day. I found myself walking on the soft cold sand and thinking about my many deaths. I could feel the pulsating air every time a wave would break upon the receiving sands. I felt the time approaching, sensing a sudden coolness in the air, a vibrant voice calling me. A voice that seemed to come from the sea, soft yet demanding my presence. I stopped and slowly looked out. A black aura seemed to hang from an invisible hand, yet, "yes, I can see you!"
> "I see you," I cried.
> The voice was coming from deep within me.
> Afraid? No, I think not.
> A new life is about to emerge.

Who will I be this time?
Everything is ghostly black now, thinking, thinking, who
this time? Mind is swirling, going deeper, deeper I go.
Strange sensation coursing through me, I'm losing old
form, dizzy, getting very yellow outside. I feel it, very
strong now, like a . . . yellow bauble . . . Death!

Upon first reading, the words do have a certain amount
of charm. However, in the analysis of the little bit of
prose, one becomes aware of the almost overwhelming
thought of death which has been planted in the man's
mind. He, through the use of automatic writing, turned
out page after page of prose, all dominated by a death
theme.

The man's conversations also became death-oriented.
Suicide became the predominant thought in his mind.
Only by finally admitting that the words were coming
through another channel and were not his own, was he
able to break the influence of the entity which had been
using him.

In the inward search for the Voice of Silence it is
possible to encounter all means of distractions. As the
spiritual centers are opened in meditation, and the kundalini begins its upward flow to the master gland, many
things are thrust in the way of the seeker; things which
are meant to sidetrack the original purpose of the search.

As we have learned, visions and scenes begin to appear
during meditation. Some of them are so lovely that one
can very easily be lead in the wrong direction, forgetting
that he is to go on beyond these distractions. One may
even consciously seek visions, among other things, mis-
taking them for the real purpose of meditation.

All should be cautioned, "Study oft how ye may interpret those visions, those activities that are gradually becoming more and more a part of thy experience; by entering into meditation. Not by attempting to write, not by attempting to hear, not by other than going within.

"For, His promise is that in the temple—in thy temple —He will meet thee—in the holy of holies. And thy body is the temple of the living God. There He will meet thee." (2560-1)

DRUGS AND MEDITATION

Frequently individuals who are on various drugs describe great spiritual experiences which they have had while on a "trip." The drug-induced experiences are very real to the one who has had them. He has seen the colors and they are unbelievably beautiful, defying all logical description. He has heard sounds which have caused pure ecstasy in his mind. He has smelled fragrances such as one could not obtain from a bouquet of a hundred full-blown roses. He has enjoyed a walk with Christ and all of His angels.

The drug-induced visions can exceed the beauty of anything anyone has ever known, and they can be equally terrifying. There is a very good possibility that they are sometimes interpretations of childhood teachings which have been locked away within the unconscious. The drugs serve as a means of releasing things which the undrugged mind would never dream of attempting to disturb. The visions are not usually the result of a spiritual meditation but are caused by the forces which have been attracted while an individual was on drugs.

To attempt to enter into meditation while on drugs can be a dangerous experiment. The mental body may be harmed beyond recall. And over a period of time the physical body is sure to break. "So seldom is it considered by all, that spirituality, mentality, and the physical being are all one; yet may indeed separate and function one without the other—and one at the expense of the other." (307-10)

The hallucinogenic drug, lysergic acid diethylamide (LSD), has been the means of causing classic cases of severe schizophrenia among a number of individuals who have used it. Unfortunately for some of those who have attempted the drug route of reaching the Christ Consciousness within, it can be misleading.

The physical-mind is a very tricky element, quite capable of leading an individual astray. Visions and other experiences can be imagined to the extent that they become almost tangible. Whatever one desires to experience can be manifested in the mind. To attempt this means of visioning is misleading and can be the means of putting many a stumbling block in the path of the searcher.

For, as has been explained, "The pattern is given thee in the mount. The *mount* is within thine inner self. To visualize by picturizing is to *become* idol worshipers. Is this pleasing, with thy conception of thy God that has given, 'Have no other Gods before me'? The God in self, the God of the universe, then meets thee in thine inner self. Be patient, and leave it with Him. He knoweth that thou hast need of before ye ask. Visualizing is telling

Him how it must look when you have received it. Is
that thy conception of an All-Wise, All-Merciful Creator?
Then, let rather thy service ever be, 'Not my will, O God,
but Thine be done in me, through me.' For all is His.
Then, think like it—and, most of all, act like it is." (705-2)

Under the influence of several different drugs, including LSD, some people change their sense of time. For
example, if they are told to tap their foot at a given rate
of speed and to do so in an even manner, they will lose
their sense of time and tap fastest at the peak of the drug
state. In all probability, it is during this time-expansion
period that those who are spiritually seeking have their
experiences and are inclined to believe that they have
experienced the true Christ Spirit.

Many of those who are sincerely in search of the Christ
within and without, and who have been fortunate enough
to survive the drug route with body and mind intact,
come to realize that spiritual meditation is the safer and
surer way of reaching the Divine within.

For it is ". . . in such a manner may individuals become aware of the Christ Consciousness and become one
with the operative forces of the Christ Spirit abroad in the
earth; for He shall come again, even as ye have seen Him
go. *Then* shall the Christ Spirit be manifest in the world,
even as the Christ Consciousness may make thee aware
of that promised as the Comforter in this material world.

"Then, the Christ Consciousness is the Holy Spirit, or
that as the promise of His presence making aware of His
activity in the earth. The Spirit is as the Christ in action
with the Spirit of the Father." (262-29)

Once individuals have learned to accept as factual that

the Spirit of the Father can act through the Christ Consciousness within, much more understanding will open up for all. There will no longer be the need for drugs and mind tranquilizers in the search for inner peace and knowledge.

Man now realizes that there is much more to the universe than that which can be detected throught the use of the known five senses. And science is slowly inching its way into the world of the unknown but its full acceptance seems to be in the distant future. Man apparently knows very little of the unseen forces, yet he is daily affected by their action. This lack of knowledge is due largely to superstition and our fear of the real truth.

Individuals are making discoveries about themselves and the unseen forces every day. Newspapers and periodicals can testify to the fact that the discoveries are not always of a constructive nature.

In the act of possession by a seemingly discarnate entity, we have learned of a young man hovering on the brink of insanity. Through the use of automatic writing, one learns that there are individuals who are driven beyond their normal way of thinking as a result of unseen forces which they have attracted.

Possession is only one way of dark forces taking hold of an individual's personality. There are a number of other ways. Too many people have had contact with drugs and realize what they can do to man's free will; many of these individuals are now searching for answers through meditation.

I am not trying to frighten anyone away from meditation; quite the contrary. I am trying to make each person aware that there are unseen forces which can be manifested through the misuse of meditation and the opening of the seven spiritual centers without the proper knowledge of handling them.

If one adheres to the spiritual preparations for meditation, such as the cleansing of the mind, ideals and affirmations, and surrounds self with the protection of the Father, there is no reason why anyone should encounter unwanted forces. It is in the neglecting of these things that individuals have difficulties.

"This is not belittling the seeking of knowledge, neither is it advising individuals . . . to seek knowledge. But knowledge without the use of same still remains, as in the beginning, sin. And be sure your sins will find you out!" (3428-1)

Chapter IX

CREATIVE TALENT AND DECISIONS

Artistic creativity is a manifestation of a gift from the highest Creator of all. It is earned by certain individuals but meant for the enjoyment and betterment of all people. To abuse, or misuse, such a gift is to trespass against the Giver of all natural gifts. Knowledge and ability not used is a sin. This applies not only to an artist capable of creating a painting which could hang in a great museum but even to miners with the ability to dig coal from the very bowels of the earth.

"He that hath *little* in experience, of him little is expected. He that hath *great* knowledge, understanding and experience, *of* him *much* is required. *Use*, then, that thou hast in hand for the service as will give the better understanding to others, and the contentment within self of the experience being well used, and made useful in the experience." (2708-1)

To attend a concert, stroll through a museum, or look

out over a field of corn waving in the sun is to become aware of the hand of God at work through the efforts and abilities of man. "That from the beginning there have been such [divine] influences upon the mind of man is seen not only in that termed Holy Writ, but also in art, in music, in song, in verse, in prose. It is demonstratable in every walk of life, and has been through all ages." (5752-4)

Many of the Cayce readings suggest that there is a close relationship between artistic creativity and the psychic. Webster defines "psychic" as "pertaining to the soul." Therefore, reason must tell us that creativity is associated with the soul of man and has to come directly from the Creator.

It is also safe to reason that creativity is heightened by contact with the Creator of the soul. And it is during meditation that creative guidance may be sought. The creative artists work best when they recognize that they are able to go within for direction and strengthening of their talents.

Creative artists often speak of their Muse, or inspiration. It is said that William Faulkner could write only so long as the "voices" spoke to him. When the voices ceased, the work was put aside until another day when Faulkner again could hear them. Wagner, the great composer, is said to have had the need to "hear" music before he could actually compose and write it.

There is scarcely anyone who has not read or heard of *Jonathan Livingston Seagull,* that wonderful bird who realized that there is so much more to life than merely hunting for food and getting through each day. The story came to Richard Bach, the author, in a vision and through a "mysterious voice." Mr. Bach believes completely in the voice and does not attempt to explain its origin.

Apparently the more developed the spirit-body becomes, the more intense is the creativity. And, as we know, in spiritual growth, individuals draw ever closer to the Giver of gifts.

"For, know that all thy attributes and activities of the senses are the gifts of God. This is true with every entity . . . For he that sings, he that sees, he that speaks, he that hears well is especially GIFTED of God . . ." (622-6)

An explanation of that particular reading says, "It was meant what was said. Just as that indicated in the parable of the talents by the Master. He that used the five talents was given more. He that uses the five senses—as of speech, of song, of hearing—to the GLORY OF GOD—is given the ten to use or rule over—as was the man with the talents." (622-7)

As creative talent is used for the betterment of God and man, more will be given.

Before any work of art can be created, the inception of the idea must be born within the artist. When one looks up at the ceiling of the Sistine Chapel in Vatican City, one gazes in wonder and has difficulty imagining how Michelangelo could possibly have envisioned this magnificent work of art. Where did the first germ of the image come from?

"The abilities in the *psychic* forces (psychic meaning, then, of the mental *and* the soul) doesn't necessarily mean the body until it's enabled to be brought into being in whatever form it may make its manifestation—which may never be in a material world, or take form in a three-dimensional plane as the earth is; it may remain in a fourth dimensional—which is an idea! Best definition that ever may be given of fourth dimension is an idea! Where will it project? Anywhere! Where does it arise from? Who knows? Where will it end? Who can tell? It is all-inclusive! It has both length, breadth, heighth and depth—is without beginning and is without ending! Dependent upon that upon which it may feed for its sustenance, or it may pass into that much as a thought or an idea. Now this isn't *ideal* that's said, it's idea, see?" (364-10)

If Michelangelo's idea for the masterpiece of his lifetime was of the psychic, or soul, then it must have been of Christ. And an idea can be brought into fruition or remain merely as a thought, or nothing. It depends entirely upon the individual receiving the idea as to what heights, or depths, it will be carried.

Through the practice of meditation we learn that it is possible for an individual soul-mind to commune with the Universal-Mind. It is through this conscious seeking that creative talent, as well as all things, may be intensified. We see the hand of God evident in all things, great or small.

DECISIONS

When a decision-making problem looms on the horizon, one eventually comes to a decision of some kind about it. But somewhere, in the back of the mind, there is sometimes that little nagging doubt as to whether or not the decision which one has arrived at is the best one.

There are times when one will take the problem to a friend, mulling it over and seeking advice. Of course, the advice which will be given is going to be based upon the friend's way of handling similar situations. One comes away still unsure about the way he had dealt with the problem in question.

Also, the personal ego is inclined to get in the way and one will have a tendency to wonder what others will think about the way he is handling the situation; how his actions will be judged. However, when one has learned to accept the fact that each person is an individual soul linked to the Creator of all souls, and He, and He alone, is the One to take all problems to, how much more sure all aspects of life become.

Failure and wrong decisions can result when one fails to recognize that He is ever waiting to council and guide all who will go within to listen and learn the answers. "For, the answer to every problem, the answer to know His way, is ever within—the answering to that real desire, that real purpose which motivates activity in the individual.

"These appear at times to become contradictory, of course; but know—as the illustration has been used here —attunement, atonement and at-onement are ONE; just as the inner self is that portion of the infinite, while the self-will or personality is ever at war with the infinite within—for the lack of what may be called stamina, faith, patience or what not. Yet each entity, each soul, knows within when it is in an at-onement." (2174-3)

With the world conditions as they are today, individuals often find themselves asking how to keep the spiritual ideals and still have the material conditions fall into their proper perspectives. This may be done by "disregarding the material conditions, let the spiritual be the guide—and the *material* will take their place.

"For, as has been given, take no thought of the morrow or of material things, for of such things do the unbelievers seek; but if ye will seek the Lord while He is nigh, all these things will be added unto thee in their proper time and place." (288-37)

It is not always easy for the mental and physical bodies to turn their very being over to the spiritual body and through it be guided. There will tend to be a constant conflict between these bodies until they begin to harmonize as one.

The more persistently one meditates, the easier it becomes to accept the decisions he makes as being the right ones for him. Eventually one does learn and understand that he can turn his life back to the Master and He will guide him in all things.

When confronted with difficult situations, it is only natural that an individual will question the decisions he makes. Is it really from the Christ Consciousness within or is it of his own desiring? This particular dilemma will be answered "As the body recognizes, there is the soul-mind, the body-consciousness, there is also the inner consciousness or soul-mind. Ask the question in self in the physical mind so it may be answered yes or no, and in meditation get the answer. Then closing self to physical consciousness, through the meditation, ask the same question. If these agree, go ahead. If these disagree, analyze [thine] own self and see the problem that lies in the way." (5091-2)

Once one has learned to trust the decisions which come with meditating on a problem, he learns it is possible to get the answer "On any subject! Whether you are going digging for fishing worms or playing a concerto." (1861-12)

Through the practice of daily meditation, one will gradually become aware of the guidance of the Christ Spirit in everything he does. He is no longer a mythical, uncaring God-figure but is as real as one's next-door neighbor. However, the outward appearance of many individual lives at times tends to lead to spiritual confusion, and one may still find himself questioning his faith and wondering if everything is going to turn out all right. It is here that all are reminded, "Thou either believest that the Christ, God *in* thee is able to keep that He promised, or thou doubtest; for He *has* not willed that *any* should perish, but has prepared a way of understanding to all that seek and are *willing*—through faith, through patience—to trust in Him." (288-37)

Today's man is not any different from Thomas, one of Jesus's disciples. He still questions and he still doubts even after hearing the voice of the Master. For the doubters, "Ask self in thy own conscious self, 'Shall I do this or not?' The voice will answer within. Then meditate, ask the same, yes or no. You may be very sure if thine own conscious self and the divine self is in accord, you are truly in that activity as indicated, 'My spirit beareth

witness with thy spirit.' You can't get far wrong in following the word, as ye call the word of God." (2072-14)

In the practice of meditation, the individual soul-mind
makes contact with the Master-Mind. It is at this point
that the still, small voice of the Spirit of the Father may
be heard. But it is not possible to function on a daily
material plane and remain at this point of contact constantly. However, when one does return to the mental
and physical levels after meditation, he brings back with
him a radiant knowledge of what is right and what is
wrong.

When meditation is considered the means whereby
questions may be asked and answers found, it is invariably believed that the question should be of great
importance before one should ask it. Apparently this is
not necessarily so. One individual asked, "Can I find help
through meditation, or in any other way, when I must
solve vital problems, as, for instance, the sudden impos-
sibility of securing buttons?"

It would seem that everything is relevant, for the
answer was, "These are very material; yet if the life is
so lived that ye are worthy of being pointed out or shown
where and how such may be obtained, ye will find the
way." (412-15)

It should always be remembered that meditation is not
a "sometime" thing. Sitting down occasionally and closing
the eyes for a few minutes cannot be called meditation
by the furtherest stretch of imagination. Going within in
meditation and listening for the Voice is an art which one
must learn.

When the desired results do not come immediately, do

not give up. Sometimes it can be "In the spiritual and mental relationships, these—as we find—the body is on the right track; yet, as will be found necessary, be as persistent in keeping those appointments with self as the body mentally or physically is desirous of gaining the good that may come from such continued actions on the part of self; for these are compliances more and more with spiritual and natural laws. Do not allow self, or the activities in this direction, to become mere rote or routine; for one will not find lest they seek, nor will one have the door open lest they expect same. As has been given, when such periods come, be consistent and persistent as results are desired; for these will gradually bring those periods in the meditation, while secular things may present themselves to the physical-mental, then when the answer is yes or no present same the second time—not to the mental being; rather ask the Spirit; for 'Will ye be my people, I will be your God' saith the Lord of hosts. Keep, then, that thou hast vowed unto thy God, to thyself, to thy neighbor." (275-87)

As one begins to accept the certain knowledge of the Christ Consciousness within, he will also begin to wonder whether the decisions are of a selfish or unselfish nature; are they for the best benefit of all concerned? The answer might well be, "As to what has motivated and does motivate the desire. If it is for the self, or for the glorification of the Christ Consciousness in thine experience. That this or that may appear to self as being well, if such and such an experience were thine own. But, as has been given, each soul may find in self an answer to that it seeks or desires to *know* from what source it (the desire) has originated, or is in its impelling force. First ask self in the physical consciousness, and answer—and find an answer—yes or no. Then enter into the inner self through meditation and prayer, and seek the answer there; for, 'My Spirit beareth witness with thy spirit as to whether thou art the sons of God or not,' in thine activity, thine desire, thine purposes, thine aims." (262-64)

————————

Chapter X

SPIRITUAL GROWTH

All who learn to meditate, whatever may be the original reason, eventually turn to the spiritual aspects of it. It is only through the spiritual that one can hope to achieve the results which lead to a fuller life for an individual. And daily meditation cannot possibly be practiced without spiritual awareness and growth slipping into the consciousness, however subtly.

The influences of spiritual activity emanate from within an individual. "And as there are the communications with the divinity within self for its uses or application in self's relationships to the conditions surrounding same, in meditative periods, these bring harmony, that peace, that understanding that is not gained by those who do not commune with the divine within. And these, to be sure, are the basis of *all* endeavors from the spiritual rapport of an entity. These are not only helpful but assist self or the entity to be the greater channel for helpfulness to others.

"For spirituality, as love, grows by finding expression— and being given out." (920-9)

Spirituality, or that awareness that comes with turning in during meditation, will continue to grow and flower as it is given out to others, as in love.

The growth of spirituality and love are as nothing unless they are shared with others. This does not mean saying one thing and doing another, but it does mean that they, spirituality and love, must permeate every cell of the body and mind and become a way of life, as vital to living as breath itself.

Spiritual growth is very closely aligned with the search for Truth. And we know "That which is truth is that which makes for an unveiling, or the making aware in the experience of any soul its relationship with Spirit or Creative Force." (275-31)

Spiritual awakening may also be equated with an individual's ability to know certain truths without consciously knowing how he knows them. The nearer one draws to the Christ Consciousness, the more likely it is that spiritual realization will take place. And with the awakening comes knowledge and tranquillity.

Bearing in mind that all the knowledge acquired during meditation does not necessarily come through the Creative Force, it is recommended that everything be carefully analyzed and studied before acceptance. The acceptance of none other than the Christ Spirit is the only answer to that which is sought during meditation.

As given earlier, "regarding those influences that are

active upon the soul consciousness of an entity when it meditates deeply, unless there are those preparations within self for the proper attitudes there may be brought [about] such influences that become detrimental to the *physical* attributes and make a mis-comprehending of that soul development which is the birthright and privilege of each soul in a material world." (436-3)

Through the study and practice of meditation, individuals have learned that they must turn within if they are to set their feet upon the path which leads to spiritual growth and self-realization. The search is stimulated by the soul's ever-constant yearning to be reunited with its Creator, for, ". . . the soul never forgets and that which is practiced to the soul, in the soul, will bring eventually a growth in the knowledge, in the understanding of the love of the Creative Forces." (5335-1)

Knowledge and spiritual growth are not going to come from the outside. Only by shutting out all else and going within during meditation does one actually become aware of that which he is trying to find.

To a degree, deep prayer and meditation involve transcending the physical and mental senses. It is in this complete unawareness of all physical things that one may become attuned to the Christ Consciousness within. Once this has been experienced, everything else then falls into its proper perspective. Do not be misled, though. Unless the knowledge and growth are used, they can very easily slip back into the unconscious and one will then have to begin the search over again.

The assurance of His presence is not guaranteed to remain in the consciousness. It is very much like a love affair where one must be told repeatedly that he is loved as he loves, or a nagging doubt starts to creep in. The material mind, accustomed to logical thinking, will say it is all wishful thinking, or perhaps it is the imagination playing tricks.

Doubt does not pick chosen ones to haunt but comes to all who seek and search for Truth, knowledge, and spiritual growth. The white light, or the manifestation of the Christ Consciousness, can be revealed in all of its glory and before many days have passed one will begin to wonder if he really did have the experience and enlightenment.

To be ever aware of the Presence, one must get it, ". . . well set in the mind. *Seeing* it, close self—mind, eyes, ears—to the outside world, recognizing as a fact, 'If I would know, if I would comprehend, I must *open* my inner self—not the *outer* self—to those influences!' And . . . the awareness flows in." (257-170)

By knowing the Father through turning within during daily meditation, by the abiding of His laws, by the giving out of love and concern for one's fellow man, does the spiritual growth come to every individual.

As He has promised, "'If ye love me ye will keep my commandments, and I and the Father will come and ABIDE with thee; and what ye ask in my name—BELIEVING—shall be done in the body.'

"These may appear in the first premise to be mere statements. But consider for the moment the conditions in which these were given, and how they may apply to thyself, in the body, now.

"First we find there is the body, the mind, the soul.

Ye may say, 'Yes, I know the body—I experience the mind—I know not the soul.'

"The SOUL is that which is the image of the Maker, and only in patience—as the Christ gave—may ye indeed become aware of thy soul's activity; through its longings, through its convictions; through its experience into the realms of the spiritual undertakings.

"How do these come about?

"Then how do they apply in thyself?

"As ye have been taught, as ye are aware, The Godhead is the Father, the Son, the Holy Spirit. Just as in thyself—as the pattern—the body, the mind, the soul. They are one, just as the Father, the Son, the Holy Spirit are one. They each, functioning in coordination or cooperation as one with another, become as thy own experiences in a material world, the awareness of the consciousness of that God-force, that Spirit abiding within.

"Then, there has been given, there has been shown the way that the Father is mindful of His children; that these as they appear in the earth—yea, thyself—are a portion of His manifestation. Not as an indefinite force, not as an unconcrete thing, not as just a mist, but just as is manifested not only in the Christ but as manifested in thee—thy desires to do right, thy desires that there be the manifesting of love, of patience, of hope, of longsuffering, of brotherly-kindness, of doing good even though others speak unkindly, when others revile thee, when others say those things that in thy physical consciousness find resentment.

"But as He manifests—a portion of that Godhead that is represented in thee, as IN thy mind—then ye become aware that ye are INDEED a child of the living God, and are in materiality for those purposes of manifesting those very things that are the fruits of the Spirit in thy dealings with thy fellow man.

"For as ye measure to thy fellow man it is measured to thee again. This is an UNCHANGEABLE law! For as ye ask for forgiveness, only in those measures in which ye forgive may ye be forgiven. For are ye not seeking to be one with Him? Then only AS ye forgive may ye BE forgiven! Only AS ye show forth love may love be shown forth to thee! Ye cannot rise above that as ye measure, that as ye live. For as the expression of life IS the manifestation of that love, then in the measure as it metes so is it measured to thee.

"Know that as the Mind is represented by the Christ Consciousness, it is the Builder, it is the Way, it is the Truth, it is the Light; that is, through the manner in which the Mind is held.

"Not that it denies, not that it rejects, but that it is MADE as one with the purposes He, thy Lord, thy Christ, thy God, thy holy self, would have it be.

"Not to the glorifying of the body. For even as He, thy Lord, gave, 'I can of myself do nothing—it is as the Father worketh in and through me.'

"Then it is as the body, the mind, the spirit—the motivating forces—coordinant as one with another, WITH the divine law. Ye know the law. What is the law?

"'Thou shalt love the Lord thy God with all thy heart, thy mind, thy body; thy neighbor as thyself.' This as He gave is the whole law. There is none above that. And ye may, as He has promised, become aware in thy own consciousness of His abiding presence, by the awareness that may come to thee as ye meditate, as ye pray from day to day.

"Ask and He will give. For as ye walk, as ye talk with Him, ye may become aware of His presence abiding with thee.

"For this purpose ye came into this experience; that ye might GLORIFY that consciousness, that awareness of His presence, of His spirit abiding with thee.

"Ye give manifestations of same in the manner, in the way in which ye measure that love to others about thee day by day.

"This do, and ye will know the truth—the truth shall indeed make you free. Not condemning, not finding fault here nor there at any of the experiences; knowing that God is, and that ye must, that ye WILL, that ye MAY— and it is the glorious opportunity, the glorious promise to just to be able to be kind, to be gentle, to be patient with thy fellow man day by day!

"And the *assurance* comes within thine own self, for His promise is to meet thee in the tabernacle of thy own conscience. For as Jesus said, 'Lo, the kingdom of heaven is within YOU!'" (1348-1)

What one sees in himself, in his actions toward others, as he lives his life day by day, is the manifestation of his spiritual growth and awareness of the Spirit within. If the daily activities in all things are carried through in a loving and generous manner, there will be great spiritual growth.

The beauty of self-less development shines from within

one; it is there for all others to see and learn from. With spiritual growth comes harmony in all things.

In the attaining of spiritual growth, one must first learn the law above all other laws; love of God, love of one's self, love of neighbors. As one begins to understand that all three precepts are interrelated as part of the Oneness, greater growth will come.

"It would be well, then, for that given through these channels (on Meditation) to be well comprehended, well understood and that, in the development of self and self's abilities to associate, the soul-development influence (that may be brought into material manifestations in or through the various forces in the experience of the individual life) be well studied, well comprehended.

"And then there may be brought for self that development which is of, from and through, self's own analyzing of the Creative Energy or the spirits, or Spirit, about the Throne that is ever a dictator in the directing of that impelling the soul development of each seeker for light in His name.

"Too, in connection with same, it would be well for that which makes for the comprehending of the oneness of all force in the effects in the mental influences, in the sources of information, in the source of life, light, truth, immortality, to be comprehended, understood, in the experience of the *mental* and the *soul* body." (436-3)

Chapter XI

PSYCHIC DEVELOPMENT

Consistent meditation contributes to the development of the psychic abilities in a great many individuals. Psychic "means that of the mind presenting the soul and spirit entity as manifested in the individual mind. Then taking the phases of that force, we find all Psychic Phenomena or force, presented through one of the acknowledged five senses of the physical or material body,—these being used as the mode of manifesting to individuals. Hence we would have in the truest sense, PSYCHIC, meaning the expressing to the material world of the latent, or hidden sense of the soul and spirit forces, whether manifesting from behind, or in and through the material plane." (3744-1)

Psychic means, then, pertaining to the soul. And through the practice of meditation, the five senses are heightened and one is able to manifest, or use, his psychic ability.

Edgar Cayce was asked how many different kinds of psychic phenomena are known, and he replied, "Almost as many as there are individuals, each entity being a force, or world within itself. Those of the unseen forces become the knowledge of the individual, the power of expression, or of giving the knowledge obtained, being of an individual matter." (3744-1)

We are aware of a number of different kinds of psychic abilities. Included among the psychic abilities are:

TELEPATHY

This is the communication of impressions or thoughts from one individual's mind to that of another. This is done independently of any of the recognized channels of communication, such as radio, television, telephone, or mail.

PRECOGNITION

Here we find the advance knowledge of an impending event supernormally acquired. There are now a number of different organizations in various parts of the world where individuals, with this particular psychic ability, may register their advance knowledge or impressions. It is hoped that in time, this advance information may be used to warn people of coming disasters, such as earthquakes, floods, and things of that nature which contribute to man's unhappiness.

PREMONITION

This is very closely akin to precognition in that it is an indication, sometimes undefinable, frequently personal, of any kind of event or happening still in the future. This could be expressed as a "hunch" or "feeling" that one might have.

TELEKINESIS

This is the developed ability of an individual to cause an object to move without physically touching it.

CLAIRVOYANCE

Individuals with the heightened psychic ability of clairvoyance have the faculty of seeing scenes, events, and other things in the future or in the past. They may see individuals participating in something which is yet to come, or has already happened. Those with this gift also sometimes have the ability to communicate with spiritual matter on other planes. Frequently, through the use of clairvoyance, lost objects or people are located.

The few psychic abilities briefly described are the more commonly known and accepted ones. In all probability, many more will be discovered as man learns to accept that which he cannot see or now understand.

There are many individuals who realize the benefits which may be derived as the result of developing the psychic abilities which lie latent within everyone. Also, they would like to know how to better develop the abilities. The following Cayce reading will answer that question.

"Psychic is of the soul; the abilities to reason *by* the faculties or by the mind of the soul. And when this is done, enter into the inner self, opening self through the ideals of the meditation that have been presented through these channels, and surrounding self with the consciousness of the Christ that He may guide in that as will be shown thee . . . or in the intuitive forces that come from the deeper meditation, may there come much that would guide self first. Do not seek first the material things, but rather spiritual guidance, developing self to the attunement of the psychic forces of the spheres as through the varied activities in the varied planes of experience, but ever in the light of that promise that has been given to be known among men, 'If ye love me, keep my commandments, that I may come and abide with thee and bring to thy remembrance those things that thou hast need of that have been *between* me and thee since the foundations of the world!'" (513-1)

Meditation is the surest and safest way to develop psychic abilities, for it is then that one is in attune with the Christ Consciousness, and it is then that the soul forces within are awakened. It is through the awakening of the soul forces that the seemingly unknown is most frequently made known.

It is during meditation, in the stilling of the physical

mind and body, that the psychic abilities are allowed to emerge from the subliminal, or from below the level of conscious knowledge. Once the spirit of the Christ Consciousness has been allowed to penetrate the level of consciousness, the barrier separating an individual from all knowledge gets thinner and thinner until it no longer exists. The past, present, and future become as now.

USE OF PSYCHIC ABILITY

"Psychic forces cover many various conditions, depending upon the development of the individual, or how far distant the entity is from the plane of spirit and soul." (3744-1)

Each individual must determine for himself the manner in which psychic ability will be applied, or even if he is desirous of developing it. Psychic ability is, as with all things, under the influence of free will, which is God-given.

Therefore, "Know that thy mind is the builder, and that it is true, as given in the days of yore, that TODAY —NOW—there is set before thee good and evil, life and death—CHOOSE THOU!

"For with the will, that is the heritage of each soul, thou choosest that which is to bring harmony or peace, or destructive forces with their attributes of every nature.

"Then weigh them in the balance of thy own conscience, in the light of that for which thy own mind and body calls. For no one CAN, no one MUST make those choices BUT SELF!" (1632-2)

One must decide why he would desire to develop psychic ability, or to see beyond the known. If it is for self-gratification, do not tamper with unknown forces. If the acquired ability is to be used for the betterment of others, decide how this is to be done before proceeding along the path of knowledge.

All who are interested in developing psychic ability must "Take council with soul, and let this be as thy first experience in thine psychic self; for psychic, as given, is but a name, yet its metes and bounds take hold upon the mental, the material and the spiritual things in the experience of every soul! But ask in self, 'What *is* my purpose? What is my inner desire? Is it an experience that I may exalt my inner self? or that I may glorify my Maker, my Redeemer, my Lord, my Master?' And get the answer from the mental self! Then enter into meditation, in the wee hours of the morning, when the world at large is quiet—when the music of the spheres and the morning stars sing for the glory of the coming day, and then ask the soul; and let the spirit of self answer. Audibly? Yea, within thine own heart will come the answer yea or nay." (440-4)

Psychic phenomena are a reality, often spontaneous and sometimes unexplainable. They may be frightening if one is not aware of the meaning and source causing the particular experience. Psychic phenomena go deeper than the physical mind, on into the soul and who knows how far beyond.

Psychic ability should not be experimented with out of curiosity, nor should the development of it be hoarded and used for selfish means. For, "that knowledge of all universal force that may be obtained through the psychic force is that of man's individual condition to be dealt with. All force that may be obtained from such source, and not used as self-aggrandizement, or for the selfish purposes of the physical attributes, may be, should be, used and given to the world.

"The understanding of all laws, for that is the law, the understanding of the law pertaining to any given condition. Then we would give any condition that may be met through such knowledge without the advantage taken of another individual, through its lack of such law or knowledge should be used. The use of psychic force by any individual, is only the using of the spiritual law that makes one free, but not freedom to take advantage, no more than that the Gods take advantage of the knowledge of man's weaknesses to use them as destructive forces.

"Through man, all law to the physical plane or material plane is made manifest, but the manifestation is of the compliance as made with the law. The knowledge of such gained through psychic force cannot be abused without receiving the same condition under which this puts such a condition upon the individual." (3744-1)

In working with the development of psychic ability, it would be well to bear in mind "Whatsoever a man soweth that shall he also reap."

With the development of psychic ability there should come better understanding of one's fellow man and his personal predicaments. The knowledge gained through spiritual and psychic ability should be used to help others grow beyond their present entrapments. And it should be used through the Law of Love.

OCCULT

The word "occult" seems to conjure up thoughts of witches and black magic in the minds of many individuals. And the words "psychic" and "occult" are sometimes confusing to those who are newly familiar with them.

"[In] the truest sense, 'psychic' [means] the expression to the material world of the latent, or hidden sense of the soul and spirit forces, whether manifested from behind, or in or through a material plane." (3744-1) Occult forces are the channel through which the soul forces manifest.

The difference between intuitive (psychic) forces and the occult, and how they might aid an individual in his development are explained thus: "From experience of an entity's whole being do the intuitive forces arise, while *occult* forces *are* those activities as a whole. Then, intuitive forces are developed more by the introspective activities of a conscious mind, until it is able to bring to bear such experiences of the entity as they act *upon* those *necessary* actions as *present* themselves in one's daily experience. *Individuals* (Now, this is well for all to learn!) *often* call this *entering* into the silence. Hence the *ability* of those of *any* cult, or any group of people who by constant introspection through entering into the silence, are *able to bring* to the surface the activities of the entity as a whole. Hence they are called sages, lamas, or such. These, when they are *made* to be what is *commonly* termed *practical*, yet remaining spiritual in aspect (that is, sticking to the truth!), they become masters. When they are turned to channels that are to *induce* influences over individuals because they have that ability to *hold* an individual, then they *abuse*. Hence the entity in its study may make for self, through the study of occult forces, by introspection, or entering into the silence, apply same in the life—see? This is opening a deep subject! And well that the entity be well *grounded* in, not as *mystics*—nor as mysterious individuals have given; know the basis of introspection, which is—in that termed *Christian* religion—prayer, while that termed in many a cult as introspection, meditation, mysticism, or occult influences brought in. They are one and the same in their essense, but *know* they are all of one source, or application. Then, [if] they are good—[they] must come from the *source* of good; and, as the Son came *from* the Father, they *are* in Him, and the *approach* to the source is *through* Him—and there is no other!" (282-3)

Intuitive ability, psychic ability, or any of the abilities as may be manifested through the occult, may be developed through the turning within during meditation. But the deciding factor is the USE of the abilities by an individual. The misapplication or misuse, of psychic abilities must be met at some time or other. To use the abilities for the purpose for which they were meant—the betterment of man—is to contribute to soul or spiritual growth in self and others.

Chapter XII

HEALING

Spiritual healing is often spoken of in hushed tones, with an undertone of the mysterious creeping in. Instant cures are sometimes referred to as miracles. Medical science frequently raises its eyebrows and looks in the other direction, perhaps hoping it will go away.

Spiritual healing is not a miracle nor is it mysterious. It is a very natural experience. It is the positive use of the creative energy flowing through an individual as a result of prayer and meditation. Spiritual healing does not necessarily have to be just physical; it can be emotional or mental, or even spiritual.

The ability to be healed or heal another can be brought into existence through prayer and meditation. "For, know that all HEALING—whether it be through the application of mechanical, mental, or spiritual forces—comes from the one source. For it is indeed as He has given, 'In Him ye live and move and have thy being.'" (1861-5)

The latent ability to heal self or heal another lies within everyone. Some have recognized the gift and have developed it to a higher degree than others. For, some care not whether these things exist. Also, there are instances when the desire to *not* be healed lies buried within the subconscious, perhaps as a part of a karmic pattern carried over from some other time in the earth. This, then, must be worked out in another manner.

Each individual who seeks healing aid must ask. "As of old, he that would be aided must seek—even as has been indicated. As has been given, let all things be done in order. Seeking, knowing—as ye measure, as ye act in thought, in mind, in heart, in body, and the imaginations of thine self become *materialized* in other's actions." (281-2)

Healing may take place when one has attuned self to the divine within, mentally surrounding that which is afflicted with the healing light of protection of the Christ Consciousness. The simple, but deeply meaningful, affirmation of "God's will be done, not my will" is most appropriate in a healing meditation.

In the visualization of the protective light around the area, or individual, in need of healing, the energizing vibrations of healing are directed to the area. In healing, one must have faith and expect that the will of the Father will be done. Spiritual healing is making use of the same vibratory power as that which was used by Christ and His disciples.

"Vibration is, in its simple essence or word, *raising* the Christ Consciousness in self to such an extent as it may flow *out* of self to him thou would direct it to. As, 'Silver

and gold I have none, but such as I have I give unto thee.'
'In the *name* of Jesus Christ stand up and walk!' *That* is
an illustration of vibration that heals, manifested in a
material world. What flowed out of Peter or John? That as
received by knowing self in its entirety, body, mind, soul,
is one *with* that Creative Energy that is LIFE itself!"
(281-7)

The *spoken word* carries the highest vibrations of all,
even greater than the vibrations of hearing and seeing.
When one prays aloud, rather than to oneself, the vibratory pattern of spiritual healing is intensified. Edgar Cayce
explains spiritual healing and the motion of the spoken
word thus:

". . . the body-physical is an atomic structure subject
to the laws of its environment, its heredity, its *soul* development.

"The activity of healing, then, is to create or make a
balance . . .

"If in the atomic forces there becomes an overbalanc-
ing, an injury, a happening, an accident, there are certain
atomic forces destroyed or others increased . . .

"When a body, separate from that one ill, then, has so
attuned or raised its own vibrations sufficiently, it may
—by the motion of the spoken word—awaken the activity of the emotions to such an extent as to revivify,
resuscitate or to change the rotary force or influence or
the atomic forces in the activity of the structural portion,
or the vital forces of the body, in such a way and manner
as to set it again in motion.

"Thus does spiritual or psychic influence of body upon
body bring healing." (281-24)

One sees, then, that all ailments are a disarranging, or destroying, of the atomic structure of a certain part of the physical body, or mental or spiritual bodies. To bring about healing means that the one being used as the channel is instrumental in the atoms returning to their healthy, or normal, positions.

One must realize that it is not himself who is the healer, but that he is allowing himself to be used as a channel through which the healing strength is being funneled to another. And it is during meditation that the healing power may be raised. "As we have indicated for the body, all healing—of every nature—MUST come from the spiritual. It is the attuning of same to the divine within self that brings healing forces. Thus, as was given, it is well that the body raise that awareness, that spiritually energizing force, consciously within self, in deep meditation; provided there IS the consciousness of what it, the influence, is to do, and this not IN its activity of a selfish nature. It may be personal, yes,—but individual more than personal." (1861-11)

The answer to a call for help is well illustrated from a personal experience in my own life. On November 3, 1970, my doctor called to say that I had a deep, penetrating duodenal ulcer. He wanted to see me immediately.

Prior to that date, I had been feeling progressively worse for about a month, with severe pain in my stomach and even more so in my back. I had finally called my doctor and described the symptoms of my illness. His nurse made an appointment for me to see a radiologist for X rays before going in for a consultation with my own doctor.

Both doctors, upon viewing the X-ray plates, agreed that I needed medical treatment at once. My doctor prescribed a diet, said I was to cut down drastically on cigarettes and that I was not to have alcoholic beverages of any kind. I was also given several prescriptions for different medications.

I took one look at the diet, got as far as puréed peas, and threw it in the wastebasket. For about a week I tried to stay on the medications, but my business schedule was quite hectic at the time and it was extremely difficult.

Approximately ten days after the diagnosis, I became acutely ill. Severe pain started on a Friday evening; by Sunday I was convinced that I was dying. I have never known such pain. Sunday night I rolled and tossed on my bed, unable to find a position that was comfortable. At one point, I called a friend. I didn't say that I was ill, but I did want to be sure that I could reach someone should an emergency develop, such as hemorrhaging.

Somehow I managed to get through that night. I went to the office on Monday morning but came home in the early afternoon.

Since I had become ill, I had stopped meditating. I suppose I was too uncomfortable to be bothered. But on that Monday evening, as ill as I was, I went into deep meditation. I don't know why; it was almost as if a power beyond my conscious control took over. I knew I had to meditate.

After meditation I went to bed and to sleep. At some point during the night I was aware of the presence of a dearly loved friend, John Hodiak, who had died about fifteen years ago.

I felt like a little child and John, the parent. He seemed to be cuddling me on his shoulder and saying, "Don't worry, honey. Everything's going to be all right, everything's going to be all right." Words of that nature were repeated to me several times, and I could physically feel his arms about me. I recall trying so desperately to wake fully, but I couldn't seem to quite make it. The next thing that I was conscious of was the playing of the alarm-radio. I felt marvelous that morning, with absolutely no indication that I had been so ill the night before.

I do not want to give the impression that it was John who had effected the cure. But I do believe that he was the intermediary, that he acted as the channel for my conscious mind to accept what was happening. I had trusted him as a close friend when he was alive and there was no reason why I should not continue to do so.

From that time until the checkup X rays on December 3, 1970, I prayed and went into deep meditation nightly. I let absolutely nothing interfere with the time I had set aside for myself each evening. And at no time did I follow the diet, nor did I ever return to the medications.

On the morning I returned to the radiologist for the X rays, he seemed slightly confused because he couldn't see the ulcer in the fluoroscope. I kept telling the poor man that I did not have an ulcer and he looked at me as if he thought I might need medical aid of another kind. He finally gave up on the fluoroscope and took me into the X-ray room.

The doctor asked me to wait while the first set of X rays were being developed. After a bit, he returned and said he would like to take another set.

My doctor's secretary later told me that the radiologist was on the phone to my doctor's office before I had the chance to leave his, the radiologist's office, demanding that the first set of X rays be returned to him immediately for comparison with the ones he had just taken.

The first X rays showed the deep ulcer. In the second set, taken thirty days later, there was no trace of an ulcer of any kind.

I prefer spicy foods and that was what I ate. I frequently had a martini, sometimes two, before lunch. And quite often a drink before dinner. I took the medications sporadically for about a week or ten days. I continued my hectic business life as president of my own public relations and advertising agency in New York. In general, I lived as I had for a number of years. Yet, one month after the first X rays there was not any trace of the penetrating ulcer which had caused me so much pain. My stomach was, and is, a healthy one.

My doctor agreed that there is only one logical answer for the healing: prayer and meditation.

I would like to remind the reader that I did not go about prayer and meditation in a haphazard manner. I have been a student of the practice for many years. Also, bear in mind that I did seek medical aid.

Many will be inclined to ask, "Is it possible for an individual to raise his own vibrations, or whatever may be necessary, to effect a self-cure?"

The answer is, "By raising that attunement of self to the spirit within, that is of the soul body . . .

"Oft in those conditions where necessary ye have seen produced within a body unusual or abnormal strength, either for physical or mental activity. From whence arose such? *Who* hath given thee power? Within what live ye? *What* is life? It is the *attuning* of self, then, to same. *How?*

"As the body-physical is purified, as the mental body is made wholly at-one with purification or purity, with the life and light within itself, healing comes, strength comes, power comes.

"So may an individual effect a healing, through meditation, through attuning not just a side of the mind nor a portion of the body but the whole, to that at-oneness with the spiritual forces within, the gift of the life-force within each body." (281-24)

In the attempt to heal self, as well as others, it is well to know and understand that the illness is not always in the part of the body seemingly afflicted. That can be the effect of a cause. And, in all probability, the actual cause can be found in seemingly unrelated areas.

If the cause can be located and healed, the effect will follow suit. "For thy body is indeed the temple of the living God. God didn't mar the body; only self can do that. By marring the mental attitudes in experiences do the physical effects come. The physical and mental attitudes, then, are to be creative; so must be the application for those things." (5326-1)

The energy vibrating through the physical body during meditation can also be of a destructive nature if not put to the proper use. The subconscious can pick up negative thoughts without one's consciously realizing it. The unconscious then finds a way to implement the negative without one's being aware that it is happening.

In September 1971 I was scheduled to go to Russia on a parapsychology field trip with a group from the Association for Research and Enlightenment. Prior to the scheduled take-off date, a number of friends and members of my own family had tried to discourage me from going. I refused to listen, but somewhere deep within my subconscious their words had taken root and were growing.

Three days before the departure date, I fell from a chair while adjusting a drape in my den. I broke one bone in my left foot and had multiple fractures in another bone.

During the few seconds of the actual fall the word "Russia" flashed through my mind. Among the first words that were said to me, even before I could pick myself up from the floor, were, "Now, you can't go to Russia."

Not only did I go to Russia, but I refused to have a cast put on the broken foot. However, I did let the osteopath bind the foot with plain surgical tape. At the time, he told me that medically there was no reason why I could not join the planned trip, but he warned me that I would spend the time in bed and that it would be a waste of time and money.

After prayer and meditation I knew that everything would be all right. I knew that I would be able to do everything that was planned. And I did. As a matter of fact, I walked a distance of about three miles one evening with the group to a theatre to see Russian films on some of the Russian parapsychology projects.

Each evening, after going to bed, I prayed and meditated, mentally surrounding the broken foot with the healing light of the Christ Consciousness. I turned the entire matter over to Christ. I prayed that there would not be any pain, and there was none.

During meditation, "There is being created that within the physical body that will have such Christ Consciousness as to eradicate all disorder." (281-5)

After the trip, I was asked by several people why I had not attempted to heal the foot. For some strange reason, which I still am not sure I understand, I felt that I should not make an attempt to heal it. I believe I had deliberately broken my foot, consciously or unconsciously, and that this was the physical effect of the negative words which had supplied the cause.

The ability to heal oneself, or to act as a channel of healing for another, lies within each individual. However, before attempting to heal another, one must first heal himself, mentally, physically, and spiritually. For, "As is manifest by the activities of those that would bring healing to others, the healing of every sort must come first in self that it may be raised in another." (281-12)

To be healed, or to act as a channel of healing for another, one must recognize that the Christ Spirit is being manifested in the act. This is the same Spirit which is sought during meditation. The latent ability to heal is reawakened when one consciously realizes that through the Christ Spirit within all things are possible.

"Even as the vibrations in self may be raised to that of the healing force as goes out from a soul to seek a union with those ills in individuals, so may self raise within self that consciousness that knocks at thine own heart—that would enter and tarry there. *Keep* that inner voice. Speak gently, speak kindly, knowing that in harmony of purpose may each add *their* part to that to be accomplished in those seeking. Those that would then be healed must seek through these channels." (281-1)

Chapter XIII

SUMMATION

Never before in the known history of the world has the growth of man's knowledge been as phenomenal as it has been in the past fifty years. Medical science is progressing by leaps and bounds. Man has walked on the surface of the moon. He has learned how to live under water for months at a time in an atomic powered submarine. These, and other things too numerous to mention, have contributed to man's knowledge about himself and his material growth.

But with all his knowledge, the eternal questions of a spiritual nature still continue to haunt man. The thirst for the answers is quite evident throughout the world today. Individuals are seeking and searching for answers in many different directions. Each one, in his own search, is discovering that the path invariably leads "within."

As a result of the knowledge and tranquillity which come with turning "within," there is a growing interest in meditation. Psychiatrists, psychologists, government-sponsored organizations, and many different religious denominations are among the many who are exploring the precepts of meditation.

The United States Army is also interested in meditation to such an extent that classes have been held at several different army posts. It is hoped that the practice of meditation will help soldiers suffering from combat fatigue and drug abuse.

With the aid of a grant from the National Institute of Mental Health of the Department of Health, Education and Welfare, meditation will soon be taught in certain high schools in the United States. There are reports coming in on some students who have been studying meditation and it seems that their grades are on the upswing, they have stopped using drugs, and they get along much better with their associates.

Also, federal prison officials are looking into the possibilities of teaching meditation to prison inmates, especially those with a long-standing record of drug abuse.

In transcendental meditation one is taught to concentrate on a sound or thought which supposedly contains the vibrations unique to that individual. This is called a *mantra* and is believed to be capable of taking the soul mind to its current level of development. The use of a spiritual affirmation, as opposed to a mantra, contributes to the growth and development of the soul. In all probability, a mantra does tend to quiet the mind, which is an achievement in itself.

Close to half a century ago, the clairvoyant readings of Edgar Cayce began to give the philosophy of meditation and the knowledge and benefits individuals might expect as the result of practicing it and its precepts. Countless thousands of individuals have, and are, practicing meditation according to what might be called the Cayce method. These people have proved the validity of it to their own satisfaction.

Through the study and practice of meditation, individuals have learned that the Christ Consciousness is within each person. The knowledge is within that all things are possible through spiritual growth. Through meditation individuals are discovering how to live in harmony with themselves and others. They are learning the meaning of "self-less development." And what it means to become one with the Creator.

In studying the Cayce readings relating to meditation, one learns that "meditation is listening to the Divine within." (1861-19) And that "It is not musing, not daydreaming, but as ye find your bodies made up of the physical, mental and spiritual, it is the attuning of the mental body and the physical body to its spiritual source." (281-41)

Individuals learn that prayer is not meant to take the place of meditation, nor is one to be confused with the other. Each has its respective place in the growth of spiritual knowledge.

A just attitude toward oneself and toward others becomes important if an individual is to reap the knowledge and growth which comes through the practice of meditation. Hindrances must be laid aside through the cleansing of the mental, the physical, and the spiritual.

The precept upon which the Cayce philosophy of meditation is based is not merely a series of random thoughts. Each and every reading has a great deal of depth which is revealed through the study of the readings. Each one is like a part of a giant puzzle, and when it is placed in its proper place, it reveals knowledge beyond what has been known to date. From the chaos of the many different techniques of meditation, the Cayce readings bring light and understanding.

As a noted Hindu told me, "The knowledge has been scattered around the world since the beginning of time like wild flowers. Edgar Cayce put it all together in one beautiful bouquet."

In the practice of meditation, the phantoms of the mind are wiped away and man knows himself for what he is; a creation of God's. In meditation, too, man begins to understand his desires and reasons for wanting to return to his Creator.

Although the approach to meditation and the results may differ, the same understanding, the same point of consciousness, and the same state of awareness are still the ultimate goals of all individuals.

During meditation, the door is opened and one knows that, ". . . 'I will bring to thy remembrance *all* that thou needest from the foundations of the world.' Who, what, how, but HIM! Who is the Maker? Who *is* the author? Who is light? Who is time? Who is space? The SON! that through His love for His brethren—for thou, thine self,—gave all that ye might have the greater, the closer communion with Him." (707-2)

BIBLIOGRAPHY

CAYCE, EDGAR

Psychic Readings, Association for Research and Enlightenment, Virginia Beach, Va.

CAYCE, HUGH LYNN

Venture Inward, Harper and Row, New York, 1964.
The Secret Place of the Most High, Searchlight, A. R. E. Press, Virginia Beach, Va., 1954.

COLEMAN, JAMES C.

Abnormal Psychology and Modern Life, Scott, Foresman and Company.

COOKE, GRACE

Meditation, The White Eagle Publishing Trust, Hampshire, England.

DALIA LAMA OF TIBET, the xivth

The Opening of the Wisdom Eye, The Theosophical Publishing House, 1972.

GOLDSMITH, JOEL S.

The Art of Meditation, Harper and Row, New York, 1956.

GRAY'S ANATOMY

JOHNSON, RAYNOR C.

The Spiritual Path, Harper and Row, New York, 1971.

Metaphysical Bible Dictionary
Unity School of Christianity, 1931.

NARANJO, CLAUDIO, and ORNSTEIN, ROBERT E.
On the Psychology of Meditation, The Viking Press, New York, 1971.

Search for God, Books I and II
Association for Research and Enlightenment, Virginia Beach, Va., 1950.

SECHRIST, ELSIE
Meditation—Gateway to Light, A. R. E. Press, Virginia Beach, Va., 1964.

SMITH, BRADFORD
Meditation: The Inward Art, J. B. Lippincott Company, 1972.

SUGRUE, THOMAS
There Is a River, Holt, Rinehart and Winston, Inc., New York, 1942.

WALLACE, H. RHODES
How to Enter the Silence, L. N. Fowler & Co., Ltd., London.

WILHELM, RICHARD
The Secret of the Golden Flower, Harcourt, Brace & World, Inc., 1969.

O23